Darkness and Light

Justice, Crime and Management for Today

by
David Faulkner

"*It was the best of times, it was the worst of times, it was the age of wisdom, it was the age of foolishness, it was the epoch of belief, it was the epoch of incredulity, it was the season of Light, it was the season of Darkness, it was the spring of hope, it was the winter of despair, we had everything before us, we had nothing before us ....*"

Charles Dickens
A Tale of Two Cities

The Howard League for Penal Reform

The Howard League

PREFACE

The appearance of this paper, *Darkness and Light*, is especially timely. During the last four or five years questions of criminal justice have increasingly been shaped for narrow political advantage. Calm reflection and due consideration of rational and humane considerations have become all too rare. For many politicians, the perception of being 'soft' on crime has to be avoided at all costs. This populist approach to criminal policy is especially evident with the run-up to the general election. Both the main political parties have set out their stalls. Towards the end of March the Labour Party's *Honesty, Consistency and Progression in Sentencing* (a paper for the PLP Home Affairs Committee) appeared, and was followed within days by the much trailed white paper, *Protecting the Public*, which detailed the Government's legislative proposals, including mandatory minimum sentences.

It is the Howard League's view that the contemporary discourse on crime and criminal justice has insufficiently addressed the underlying principles or the fundamental choices as to the values at stake. In our early thoughts about a Howard League paper we were greatly encouraged by David Faulkner's ready agreement to take on the burden of drafting. Currently a member of the Howard League Council, David Faulkner was deputy-under-secretary at the Home Office with responsibility for criminal policy from 1982-1990. His name is rightly associated with concerted attempts to create a principled sentencing framework, the encouragement of social crime prevention and for the support which he gave to research activities within and beyond the Home Office. While David Faulkner is the author of *Darkness and Light*, he worked closely at all stages with the Howard League's policy group and we are delighted to publish it as Howard League report.

I am confident that *Darkness and Light*, with its eloquent plea for an approach 'based on values of inclusion and high trust' will do much to reinforce efforts which attempt to ensure that policy and practice be more productive and less damaging. Its message, however, goes beyond the concerns of policy-makers and practitioners and reaches wider questions as to what constitutes a decent society.

Sir Peter Lloyd, now a member of the Howard League Council, worked with David Faulkner for a number of years at the Home Office, and we are most grateful to him for contributing the foreword to this report.

Professor Andrew Rutherford
Chair, The Howard League

The Howard League

FOREWORD

Criminal justice policy has evolved with bewildering rapidity over the last two decades. It is a story David Faulkner is well place to chronicle having spent his main career in the Home Office from 1959-1992 rising to the eminence of Deputy Secretary - experience extended and deepened by his crucial work at Oxford University's Centre for Criminological Research.

But he does more than trace the zigzag march from "nothing works" of the 1970s through the purposeful managerialism of the 1980s to "prison works" of the 1990s - the shorthand descriptions which he knows both illumine and distort what was intended as well as what actually happened.

His aim, as he says in his conclusion, is to stimulate a "thoughtful principled debate about the nature and causes of crime; the means of preventing it and mitigating the effect; the purpose, operation and effectiveness of the criminal justice process and the treatment of offenders". In fact he goes even further and with impressive clarity and economy draws on his long experience of government and thorough scholarship (the bibliography at the back from Ashworth to Zedner covers more than six pages) to set the entire criminal justice system in a social context.

It is plain from the way he writes that he is a man of Woolf and the 1991 Criminal Justice Act which as Deputy Secretary he had a central role in preparing, but as an experienced civil servant he well understands that faced by a public afraid that law and order is breaking down and a press which fans its fears, governments "must give an overriding impression of being tough on crime."

Unfortunately their spokespeople generally manage to do so in a manner that reinforces the public's belief that only a narrow punitive response can work and that efforts to humanise, help and rehabilitate are the work of unreconstructed do-gooders in the system whom Ministers are too weak to root out.

Thus government succeeds neither in reassuring the public nor in giving encouragement or leadership to those in the criminal justice system who are engaged in the government's own extensive programmes of prevention, diversion and rehabilitation, even though such programmes are the reverse of soft options and, when run properly, make heavy demands on the offender.

Virtually all criminals start young. A third of young men have a conviction by the time they are 30. Many more will have committed offences for which they were never caught.

Far fewer will become habitual criminals. Most will grow out of it sooner or later, but not until they have done their victims and themselves much damage - some of it permanent.

In Chapter V, Mr Faulkner discusses what I believe to be the most crucial question of the many he raises - how to develop specific programmes and a general environment which will help to reduce criminal tendencies in young people <u>before</u> they become offenders. The fact that such a high proportion of inmates at Young Offenders Institutions have been in care some time in their childhood intimates how fundamental a question it is - one going to the heart of family relationships in a fractured family society. There are some promising schemes in place, but more thought and experimentation are badly needed. I hope this paper will stimulate them.

I am sure *Darkness and Light* will be widely read in the criminal justice world and will influence the ideas and action there, but it needs and deserves to reach the general public too. It is a huge impediment to the country's efforts to deal effectively with crime, that criminal justice policy is so little discussed in the press and on TV. Crime itself is certainly reported in anxiety creating volume and titillating detail, but the ways society responds to it are seldom examined thoughtfully and critically as economic and foreign policies are.

In the interest of democracy and social tranquillity that gap must be closed. If it was, I do not believe for a moment that the public would cease to want to be "tough" on crime, but I have no doubt that many people would be persuaded that there were many more productive and humane ways of being tough than they had previously considered. This excellent publication by David Faulkner should help to bridge it.

The Rt. Hon. Sir Peter Lloyd MP

Darkness and Light:
Justice, Crime and Management for Today

A Howard League Paper

Table of Contents

ACKNOWLEDGEMENTS

This paper draws on material from a wide variety of sources, in several different professions, occupations and academic disciplines. Most of it is founded either in direct experience or observation, or in rigorous empirical research. Published material has where possible been acknowledged in the text; other important contributions have come from participants at conferences and seminars, and from informal talks with practitioners and academics both in this country and abroad.

Among those who have contributed directly to the text, particular thanks are due to Ros Burnett, Mark Freedland, Andrew Sanders and Lucia Zedner in Oxford; to Barry Loveday in Portsmouth; and to members of the Council, Policy Committee and staff of the Howard League, including especially Ruth Allan, Elizabeth Burney, Frances Crook, Martin Davis, Anthony Holland, Andrew Rutherford and Barry Smith. Anita Dockley deserves special gratitude, both for her contribution to its content and for her tireless efforts in supervising its production, design and distribution. None necessarily shares the views which are expressed in this paper, and any errors of fact or judgement are entirely the author's own.

I must also thank The Children's Society and Richard White, of the Thames Valley Police for generously allowing the Howard League to use their photographs for the cover design.

David Faulkner

ISSUES AND RECOMMENDATIONS

A Summary

This paper:

- Considers the level and nature of crime, and the state of the criminal justice system;

- Reviews the evidence and arguments;

- Explores a range of measures for reducing crime and mitigating its effects;

- Examines the widening range of issues which affect the management of the criminal justice system, and public services generally; and

- Suggests an approach to crime and the administration of criminal justice which will be principled, realistic and effective.

This analysis raises a number of key points, and key questions, for the future development of policy, legislation and professional practice.

Key points

Measures to reduce crime and deal with its effects cannot be left to the criminal justice process on its own. Most of the influences on crime and criminality lie elsewhere in society and must be tackled where they are to be found - especially in the experiences of childhood and the opportunities and temptations in adolescence.

The purpose of the criminal justice services should not be seen narrowly as controlling and punishing crime, but as public service in a broader sense - protecting the weak and vulnerable, promoting social stability and public safety, upholding standards of justice and civilised behaviour.

These purposes are not always best served by simply enforcing the criminal law, still less by enlarging its scope or increasing its severity. Other methods such as mediation or conciliation may sometimes be more successful. Many situations are not amenable to criminal justice solutions, and it should not be seen as a failure of the system if such a solution is not always practicable.

Victims are entitled to the dignity and respect of citizenship. They have special claims on the state and its agencies, and on their fellow citizens, for the experience they have suffered - always for information, support and sympathetic understanding; sometimes for compensation, treatment or counselling; and where necessary for protection from a repeat offence. The rights of citizenship do not, however, extend to a general entitlement to the use of force, or to personal influence over the state's decision-making process in respect of an offender. The state should not use the victim as a agent of retribution.

Criminals are not a separate class to be controlled or excluded, but fellow citizens to be brought so far as possible into a position where they too can undertake the obligations of citizenship and gain the respect of others. Many people will be both offenders and victims at different times in their lives.

Criminal justice services must be efficient and accountable. Much has been achieved in recent years, but efficiency cannot be judged only by means of internal performance indicators, without reference to external outcomes, and accountability should not be seen only in terms of financial accountability to central government. A wider vision of accountability is needed, founded on recognised principles and values and secured ultimately by legislation and the rule of law.

A country's approach to crime and criminal justice is a reflection of the attitudes and relationships within society as a whole, and is a part of its approach to wider questions of social order and justice and the nature of its institutions and organisations. The approach of a healthy and confident society will be based on values of inclusion and trust; the approach of a society which is divided and unsure of itself will be one of exclusion, suspicion and fear.

Political strength will show itself not in an obsession with punishment but in the courage to seek and analyse information, to listen to argument, and to act rationally on a basis of principle and considered judgement.

Key Questions

The priorities for the next Parliament, and the questions to be answered in addressing them, should therefore be as follows.

Support, understanding and protection of victims of crime, with respect for their status as citizens.

- ◆ Are victims' proper expectations of the criminal justice and of other statutory services - and the limits to be placed on those expectations - codified, recognised and understood?
- ◆ How should the arrangements for compensation, and the relationship between compensation and other forms of state support, be refined and developed?
- ◆ How can statutory services give a better service to victims?

◆ Should any new duties be imposed on those services? Should those duties be defined in statute?

◆ What obligations do victims have in return?

Support and guidance for children growing up in difficult circumstances and for their parents.

◆ How can support for children be most effectively stimulated, co-ordinated and sustained?

◆ What should be the responsibilities of schools, social services and primary care teams in the health service?

◆ How can purchasing decisions be suitably informed?

◆ What should be the role of the voluntary sector and how should it be funded?

◆ What are the responsibilities of parents?

◆ To what extent should they be enforced and by what means?

◆ What can be done to reverse the trend toward increasing criminalisation?

◆ How can young people themselves be involved in making decisions about these issues?

Opportunities for young people entering upon adult life and their ability to take advantage of them.

◆ How can young people, including those who have been in trouble with the law, achieve a sense of stability and hope for the future?

◆ What are the responsibilities of employers, social services, social security, the youth service and housing authorities?

◆ What is the relationship with other social and economic policies and how could policies be better co-ordinated?

◆ How can the unnecessary use of penal custody for young people be reduced?

◆ What additional facilities are needed for young people in trouble with the criminal law?

Comprehensive programmes to prevent and reduce crime at local level, effectively co-ordinated and with stable and flexible funding.

◆ How far and in what respects can the criminal justice process realistically be regarded as an effective means of reducing or preventing crime?

◆ How can the processes of detection and law enforcement be linked with programmes to reduce criminality and to improve the motivation of those at risk of offending or re-offending?

◆ What are the responsibilities of the statutory services, the business community and the voluntary sector?

◆ How can programmes be most effectively promoted, funded and co-ordinated? How can partnerships be made more successful?

- Are the proportions of public expenditure allocated to prevention and to other criminal justice activities, for instance imprisonment, correct?
- Should statutory responsibility be placed on local authorities?
- What further improvements are possible in the technology and techniques of crime prevention and detection?
- What are their limitations and what safeguards are needed for their use?

Integrity and consistent practice in the criminal justice process.

- What is the scope for increasing the number of convictions whether by new methods of investigation and law enforcement or by the use of new technology?
- What are likely to be the effect of such methods on levels of crime? Or on the operation of the criminal justice system as a whole? What safeguards might be needed?
- What issues arise from the operation of recent legislation, or from proposals for new legislation, affecting, for example the right to silence, the disclosure of the defence or prosecution case, or the rules of evidence? How are the measures already in force working in practice?
- What should be the future role of the Crown Prosecution Service, for example, in supervising and co-operating with the police investigation, sentencing or representing the interest of the victim?
- Is there a need for a change in sentencing practice, for more consistency, or for a more structured approach? How should it be achieved?
- What should be the priorities for future legislation on criminal law and criminal justice?

Programmes for offenders whose aim in giving effect to the sentence of the court is to enable them to take their place in society as responsible citizens, and to carry out their obligations and sustain their relationships.

- What are the values and principles on which programmes should be based?
- How can sentences be focused more effectively on the prevention of re-offending and on developing responsible attitudes to personal and working relationships?
- What features of those programmes and what methods of delivery are likely to be most successful? How can they be promoted and how can their success be measured?
- What are the implications for case management, risk assessment and the development of "what works"?
- How should the probation order, community service order and other community sanctions and their use be further developed?
- What is the scope for mediation, reconciliation and reparation? How could their use be expanded?
- Should the prison population be reduced and if so by what means?
- What are the implications for the structure, accountability and legitimacy of the relevant services, for their culture, and for the relationships between those services and between services and the public?

Structures and procedures designed to promote accountability, trust, a sense of strategic direction, and sound working relationships.

- ◆ What kinds of evidence, research and analysis are needed to ensure that decisions are properly informed, and their results are objectively assessed? How can they be obtained?
- ◆ What new structures will be needed?
- ◆ How should existing structures such as the Criminal Justice Consultative Council be developed?
- ◆ How can accountability to central government be combined with more plural forms of accountability, or responsibility, to organisations and individuals, including a greater sense of responsibility to local communities?
- ◆ What management procedures, and what conditions of employment, are most likely to support a spirit of public service, effective accountability and sound working relationships?

The Howard League

CHAPTER I

The Problem of Crime

The country is rightly concerned about the level and nature of crime, and about the state of the criminal justice system. Despite the welcome fall in the statistics for recorded crime, crime is seen to be a constant threat and the criminal justice system appears to be failing and in a state of perpetual crisis and organisational change. But a closer look shows that the problem is seen in different ways, in different places and by different people. The crisis is described in different terms, and the proposed solutions take different forms.

Confidence in Criminal Justice

Confidence in the criminal justice system has become an increasingly prominent theme of Government policy during the last fifteen years. Confidence may, however, mean different things to different people. For the general public, confidence is threatened if the police appear to be uninterested or unresponsive, if crime appears to be "out of control", and if offenders seem to be "getting away with it" by not being caught, prosecuted, convicted and sentenced - or if they are sentenced, because community sentences or prison conditions do not seem to be sufficiently severe or demanding. To the government, the criminal justice system may seem expensive, inefficient and ineffective, either because of supposed structural or managerial weakness, or because the professionals who manage or work in it are thought to have had too great an influence or in some instances to be unduly "liberal" in their outlook. Professionals themselves may feel undervalued, misunderstood, short of resources and constantly subjected to new legislation and demands for change. Police and ministers may perceive the system as balanced too much in favour of the offender, and therefore (it seems to follow) against the victim. Victims may feel that it gives them little or none of the recognition or respect they believe they deserve and have been led to expect, and sometimes even that they have been humiliated and betrayed. Offenders may see it as incomprehensible, unpredictable, arbitrary and capricious, but also easy to manipulate. Reformers are still concerned about actual or possible miscarriages of justice; discrimination against racial and cultural minorities, and sometimes against women; the criminalisation of children; the over-use of imprisonment and the degrading conditions which result from it; and the longer term social consequences.

Many of the views indicated in the previous paragraph are asserted vehemently and confidently by those who claim to represent public opinion, but more often on a basis of anecdote or impression than of systematic analysis or empirical evidence. Such evidence

1

as is available from surveys or from practitioners' first-hand experience suggests that the situation may often be less straightforward than it is sometimes made to appear (Walker et al 1988; Downes and Morgan 1994; Hough 1995; Victim Support 1995). But the demand for "tough" action is undoubtedly a powerful political force, with strong public support.

Nature of the Argument ...

Arguments about crime and criminal justice tend to confuse two sets of issues. One is about crime and how to prevent or reduce it, and the other is about the process for dealing with crime once it has been committed. The latter has two aspects: measures for repairing, so far as possible, the harm that has been done, and the action to be taken with or against the offender. Much of the frustration in recent argument has arisen from the assumption that crime can be reduced, and its victims can be supported, simply by action against the offender. Not only that, but action against actual or supposed offenders is sometimes seen not only as the natural response to the problem of crime and the needs of its victims, but as the only response that is seriously required.

... of the Proposed Solutions ...

The argument that the way to deal with crime is to prosecute more suspects and punish offenders more severely appeals to common sense and may sometimes be emotionally satisfying. It has a particular appeal to a managerial or consumerist approach to public services (Lacey 1994a; Sanders 1994a). All public services are quite properly required to demonstrate value for money in terms of measurable outputs, key performance indicators and satisfaction for the consumer. It is natural for a consumerist government and a cost conscious public to expect the criminal justice services to show improvements in efficiency and effectiveness, and that those improvements should be measured in terms of increased activity. It is equally natural for them to see a programme for reorganising those services or for changing the way in which they operate as a programme which will have that effect. Numbers of arrests and convictions, and even the length of prison sentences and the numbers serving them, are convenient measures of output. But crime is a complex phenomenon and criminal justice is an intricate process. Increased activity does not necessarily reduce crime and, changes in structure or procedure can have unexpected and unintended results. Much depends on the way in which the process is managed, and on the outlook, attitudes and motivation of those who are engaged in it. These attitudes are themselves influenced by the extent to which staff feel valued, confident and secure, and by the relationships which they form among themselves and with those with whom they have to work.

An approach which relies on the criminal justice process as the principal means of preventing or reducing crime, or which expects changes in that process significantly to affect the general level of crime, reflects a misunderstanding of the nature of crime, and a misapprehension of the purpose of the criminal justice process and of what can properly be expected from it. As long ago as 1829, Sir Richard Mayne and Colonel Rowan, the first Commissioners of the Metropolitan Police, distinguished between the prevention of crime and the detection and punishing of offenders as complementary but separate functions when they wrote:

> *The primary object of an efficient police is the prevention of crime; the next that of detection and punishment of offenders if crime is committed. To these ends, all the efforts of the police should be directed. The protection of life and property, the preservation of public tranquillity, and the absence of crime, will alone prove whether these efforts have been successful, and whether the objects for which the police were appointed have been attained.*

... and the Consequences

Much of the pessimism, disillusion and cynicism which has characterised some of the recent debate (Reiner and Cross 1991; Brake and Hale 1992; Downes and Morgan 1994) can be attributed to a failure to recognise the distinction between prevention and enforcement. The situation becomes even more serious if disillusion leads not to an attempt to construct more realistic and imaginative approaches to preventing or reducing crime (Braithwaite and Pettit 1990; Hudson 1993), but to simplistic demands for more repressive forms of enforcement and more severe punishment. These demands can lead in turn to a coarsening of standards not only of debate but also of justice itself.

3

CHAPTER II

The Social and Political Context

Modern societies in developed countries and countries in transition have to resolve two difficult conflicts. One is between economic progress, or economic survival, and social stability. The other is between the pressure to control crime and the need to maintain standards of justice and humanity. The first has been dealt with in, for example, Will Hutton's book *The State We're In* (Hutton 1995); the second is the subject of this volume.

Social, Economic and Institutional Change

British society is changing rapidly. Changes in patterns of employment, the development of careers, the formation of families and personal relationships are recognised and to a large extent understood, if not always accepted. Changes in public institutions - the structure of government and public service employment, and the lines of accountability - are also familiar. But the underlying or implied changes in public values, attitudes and expectations are only now beginning to emerge. Personal security, health, education and housing are becoming commodities to be purchased, not obligations to be undertaken and still less rights to be protected by the state and enjoyed by the citizen. Citizens are defined as consumers of particular public services, not as people who share a sense of common interest or identity or who are joined by any sense of mutual obligation or trust. Public service is defined by the achievement of internal targets and performance indicators rather than by social or economic outcomes. The values of public service become those of managerial efficiency, to be achieved for its own sake and not in pursuit of any wider purpose or obligation. The state, or rather the political administration of the day, becomes increasingly powerful, centralised and remote, while divesting itself of its responsibilities towards its citizens and placing those responsibilities in the hands of private or intermediate organisations with their own, often commercial or quasi-commercial, interests and objectives. These changes are usually presented as common sense, as necessary and even inevitable in a world of global markets and resource constraints, and as un-controversial and politically neutral. In fact they may have a profound effect not only on the character of public services but also on the nature of modern society, the relationships within it, and the quality of justice (Cohen 1985; 1996; Nelken 1995; Lacey 1994a; Nellis 1995; Freedland 1996).

Application to Crime and Criminal Justice

Developments in the management of organisations take on an extra dimension when they are applied to crime and criminal justice. Governments, and criminal justice services themselves, understandably define the services' objectives and targets in what they see as realistic, and therefore limited, terms. They design performance indicators which measure the services' own activity - numbers of incidents or episodes, response times, throughput - rather than outcomes such as public safety and confidence or the rehabilitation of offenders. They are in their own terms right to do so, because outcomes of this kind depend on a much wider range of factors which criminal justice services by themselves cannot control or even influence. But the consequence is that no-one is seen to accept responsibility for the general level of crime or the damage it causes. The resulting frustration finds expression in calls for severity of punishment for which there is no rational basis, and a weak administration will respond to them by imposing policies and practices which are designed without regard for their longer term consequences or the means of putting them into practical effect.

Exclusion

A separate but parallel analysis distinguishes between what might be termed an "exclusive" and an "inclusive" view of society and citizenship, again with implications for the approach to criminal justice and to the provision of services and the management of organisations. The "exclusive" view emphasises personal freedom and individual responsibility but is inclined to disregard the influence of situations and circumstances. It distinguishes between a deserving majority who are self-reliant and law-abiding and entitled to benefit themselves and those around them without interference from others; and an undeserving, feckless, welfare-dependent and potentially criminal minority - or under-class - from whom they need to be protected. The benefits of citizenship, or membership of a community, are confined to those who conform to accepted standards or who can afford to pay for them. Human behaviour is thought to be motivated mainly by a desire for material gain or by fear of punishment or disgrace. There is not much interest in, or respect for, notions of equality or social justice, or of public duty or service. A society which adopts this view is likely to be unsure of itself, suspicious of strangers, hostile towards foreigners and fearful of those who do not conform to its assumptions and stereotypes (Zedner 1995). It will favour such measures as the carrying of identity cards, the maintenance of personal records with access to them by those in authority, and the reporting of suspicious persons or events. Its decision-making processes will be cautious, closed and secretive.

Inclusion

The contrasting "inclusive" view is less commonly expressed. It recognises the capacity and will of individuals to change - to improve if they are given guidance, help and encouragement; to be damaged if they are abused or humiliated. It emphasises respect for human dignity and personal identity, and a sense of public duty and social responsibility. It looks more towards putting things right for the future than to allocating blame and awarding punishment, although the latter may sometimes be part of the former. Citizenship and membership of the community are seen as permanent attributes, and the duty to conform to society's or the community's standards is matched by the community's own obligation to support its vulnerable and disadvantaged members. The "inclusive" view is likely to be characteristic of a society which is open and compassionate, which accommodates and respects plurality, and which has some confidence in the future.

Exclusion and Inclusion in Criminal Justice

These constructions of society and organisations, and of the relationships within them, have important implications for crime and criminal justice. On the "exclusive" view, social problems can be dealt with by creating new criminal offences or increasing penalties. Punishment is seen as an instrument of social control - perhaps the only instrument that is needed - and as a means of protecting the supposedly innocent from the supposedly guilty or the deserving from the undeserving. It can be measured by its effectiveness in achieving that purpose. Crime is to be prevented by efficiency of detection, certainty of conviction and severity of punishment, including the incapacitating effect of imprisonment (Packer 1968; Reiner 1992; Sanders 1994; Lacey 1994b). "Criminals" are to be seen as an "enemy" to be defeated and humiliated, in a "war" in which the police are seen as the "front line".

On the "inclusive" view, the purpose of justice is expressed in terms such as upholding the rule of law, protecting the weak and vulnerable, expressing society's condemnation of crime and socially damaging conduct, and vindicating its victims. In the words of John Locke, *[t]he end of law is not to abolish or restrain but to preserve and enlarge freedom* (Locke 1690). People may have to be punished, but for what they have done and not for who they are (one of the underlying principles of the Criminal Justice Act 1991). The criminal law and the criminal justice process are not to be seen as the means of solving social problems, or even as the principal means of reducing crime or mitigating its effects. Solutions to the problems of crime have to be sought by inclusion within the community itself - among parents, in schools, by providing opportunities and hope for young people - and not by exclusion from it. Authority will not be respected if it is simply imposed: it has to be accountable and it has to be legitimate in the sense that respect for it has to be earned and justified. Consideration for others and obedience to the law are learned by explanation, discussion, experience and example.

Trust Within Organisations

The "exclusive" and "inclusive" views of society have their counterpart in the contrasting "low trust" and "high trust" approaches to the management of organisations (Fox 1974). The "low trust" view emphasises the discipline of competition and market forces: the threat of redundancy or dismissal; individual contracts; a top-down structure of output measures and performance indicators; compliance with rules; and material rewards, especially through performance-related pay. Not much is made of such notions as personal loyalty or mutual confidence.

The "high trust" view emphasises a participative style of management, based on negotiation, consultation and communication. It rewards teams rather than individuals and it seeks to improve and recognise good performance rather than punish failure. It values discretion and trust. Partnerships and contracts are between equals, not between superiors and inferiors or the more and the less powerful. An organisation's internal style must match the function it has to perform: if public servants, especially those in positions of authority, do not feel respected by their employing organisations or others to whom they feel accountable, they will not easily show respect for others, or receive it in return.

Citizenship, Society and Communities - A Wider Perspective

The attitudes and approaches described in this chapter should not be seen as representing a "right" or "wrong" view of society or of public policy, or as providing paradigms for public administration in general. But they do provide a frame of reference within which legislation, policy and administrative and professional practice can be examined and tested, and some insight obtained into the motivation, likely appeal, and possible consequences of proposals which may be put forward and of options which may present themselves.

An important illustration relates to the notion of "community" (Nelken 1995; Lacey and Zedner 1995). An emphasis on communities can readily be seen as an expression of the "inclusive" approach, with its implications for mutual co-operation and a sense of mutual obligation. But communities can also be defined exclusively. Communities which are most easily recognised - such as those based on culture, religion, occupation or sometimes even geographical location - implicitly exclude those who do not qualify for membership or conform to their requirements. Emphasis on communities can be used to promote the notions of self-reliance and independence, but also a sense of separation from the state and the protection and support it might otherwise be expected to provide. It can be to devalue the principles of personal freedom and procedural justice. Community sentences, care in the community and community health are often defined negatively - by the fact that they are not served in prisons, or delivered in hospitals or other institutions - rather than by any positive reference to the energy, skills, services and obligations which are to be found within wider communities, or to the means of mobilising them for the purpose in hand. The language of "communities" needs to be used with caution, and scrutinised with care (Lacey and Zedner 1995; Ashworth 1996).

CHAPTER III

Crime and Who Commits It

Crime takes different forms, and is committed in different circumstances, with different results, with different types of motivation, and by different kinds of people. Most acts which are criminal are generally perceived as wrong (for example, most forms of violence or theft); for others the fact that they are crimes at all may be seen by some people as an unreasonable encroachment on personal freedom (some regulatory and public order offences). Some criminal acts may have no obvious effects; but the same action committed in different circumstances may have appalling consequences (for example supplying an ecstasy tablet or driving under the influence of alcohol). Some offences are committed for calculated gain, some for excitement or amusement, others in moments of anger or weakness. Some acts may not be criminal but still cause distress, fear or anger ("loutish" behaviour of various kinds). A large proportion of offences are committed by young men, with a peak age of offending in their late teens (Home Office 1995a).

What Constitutes Crime

In public debate, a "crime" is usually thought of as act of violence, theft or vandalism against an individual victim or his or her home or property. These are the crimes about which most is known, which can most easily be counted and analysed, and whose consequences can most accurately be measured. This process is now carried out through the British Crime Surveys and the studies related to them (Hough and Mayhew 1983; 1985; Mayhew et al 1993; 1994; Hough 1995). The effects of such crimes are always serious and sometimes devastating, depending on the nature of the offence and the situation of the victim (Maguire 1980; Shapland et al 1985; Morgan and Zedner 1992; Zedner 1994). They can sometimes be mitigated by insurance, compensation or the support of those with whom the victim has contact, but the hurt always remains. The hurt is greater if there appears, for example, to be a racial element or if the victim appears to have been deliberately targeted as an individual. It may, possibly, be less serious if the victim can see some explanation for what has happened, and some evidence of remorse on the offender's part. But in many cases the crime remains unsolved, no offender is identified, and there is no conviction in court. Of crimes covered by the British Crime Survey, only three per cent result in a conviction in court or a caution by the police (Home Office 1995a).

Outcomes of crimes committed against individuals and their property

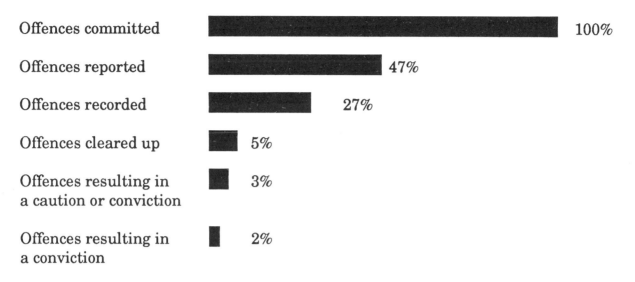

Offences committed	100%
Offences reported	47%
Offences recorded	27%
Offences cleared up	5%
Offences resulting in a caution or conviction	3%
Offences resulting in a conviction	2%

Source: Criminal Statistics: England and Wales and Trends in Crime: Findings from the 1994 British Crime Survey (Research Findings 14, HMSO)

There are many other crimes where there is no individual or direct victim, which may be undetected, but which may have equally serious consequences for businesses, local communities and the country as a whole. Theft from shops, fraud (on a large or small scale), drug offences and damage to public property are some examples (Wells 1994). Financial losses to retail businesses may be even greater than the losses to individuals, and further losses are caused to local authorities, transport operators and utilities (Speed et al 1995). Offences involving environmental pollution or danger to health and safety may have equally serious consequences, but may not be taken so seriously, especially if commercial interests are involved or jobs are said to be at risk, until a disaster occurs.

Public order offences are another, increasingly sensitive, category. They can raise important questions about the balance between civil liberties and the interests they are designed to protect, and about the wider social effects of criminalising such diverse groups as demonstrators (whether against the building of motorways, the export of live animals or fox hunting), "ravers" and "travellers" (Penal Affairs Consortium 1994f). They also raise practical questions about the relative priority to be given to the enforcement of those offences in the allocation of scarce resources.

Fear of Crime

The consequences of many crimes extend far beyond their immediate victims, whether they are individuals, businesses or organisations. Fear of crime restricts the lives of a large proportion of the population, especially the elderly but increasingly women, parents and small children (Maxfield 1984; Morgan and Zedner 1992). Although the risks may statistically be very small, and other risks, for example from accidents, may be much greater, it is hard (and arguably irresponsible) to tell a nervous pensioner that is safe to walk home alone at night, or an anxious parent that a child can safely play in the park without an adult to protect and supervise. People who are regarded as vulnerable, those who care for them, and ultimately whole communities or neighbourhoods, become nervous, isolated, distrustful of strangers and ultimately hostile towards them. Social activities are abandoned for lack of support, clubs and businesses close down, local employment is harder to find, and public transport is withdrawn. Fear of crime permeates all sections of the community.

Criminal Careers

Some experience of offending is a common part of growing up. It still comes as a surprise to many people that a third of young men have a conviction for a relatively serious ("standard list") offence by the time they are thirty (Home Office 1995a; 1995b), and many others will have committed offences but have not been caught. Self report studies, in which samples of the population are asked in confidence whether they have committed offences for which they have not been caught, suggest that crime is committed by a much larger proportion of the population than is officially held responsible for it (Maguire 1994), usually by young people. One in four males and one in eight females aged 14-25 years admitted committing an offence in 1992 (Graham and Bowling 1995). It is less of a surprise that five per cent of young men are responsible for about 60 per cent of the crime that is attributed to an offender, with an average of five or six convictions each; or that a quarter of male offenders and one in ten female offenders admitted committing more than five offences. Even that is still a lot of young people: on average, one or two boys in a class of thirty will be, or are already, relatively persistent offenders. But persistent offenders are not committing offences all the time. For most young people offending is a short episode, to be brought to an end as rapidly and with as little damage (to the young person and to the community) as possible, and better still, to be prevented altogether (Rutherford 1992).

Above all "criminals" are not a separate, identifiable group of people. Offending becomes less frequent and will usually stop altogether as offenders grow older, although a minority may continue for some time; and many offenders have been or will become victims themselves (Farrington 1994; Levi 1994; Rivara et al 1995).

11

Political Responses to Crime

Decision-makers, opinion-formers and commentators all complain, quite rightly, about the rise in crime. They will attribute it to a decline in moral standards, lack of respect for authority, the influence of the media and the ineffectiveness of the criminal justice process. They will call for changes in procedure to obtain more convictions, the creation of new criminal offences, more severe sentencing, more rigorous conditions for those under supervision in the community and harsher treatment in prisons. Children and young people, members of the ethnic minorities, and single or isolated parents are demonised (newspapers have described children as "rats" or "vermin"). The language of a "war" on crime has returned to political debate, with images of an "enemy" to be defeated and humiliated by whatever means are available.

Attitudes and demands of this kind reflect, and also reinforce, the emotions - the sense of fear, the need for protection and the calls for exclusion - which crime and the threat of crime can generate. They generate an exclusive view of crime and criminality. They can attract cheap applause. But they also reflect a distorted view of the nature and purpose of the criminal justice process and of what can be expected from it. The most vulnerable members of society, and those most at risk of offending, feel themselves the first to be denied its protection and support; and if they are also denied its respect it is not surprising that they show little in return. Those who feel that they are excluded from the benefits of citizenship cannot be expected to share in its duties and obligations (Braithwaite 1993).

Later chapters will develop this analysis and make proposals both for reducing crime and improving the operation of the criminal justice process.

CHAPTER IV

Purposes, Principles and Policies

This chapter considers the way in which criminal justice policy has developed during the last forty years, the purposes and objectives which have been pursued or assumed, and the principles which have been followed.

Aims of the System

Most people would now agree that the aims of the criminal justice system should include:

- to prevent or reduce crime;
- to reduce the fear and damage it causes;
- to support or vindicate the victim;
- to deal with suspects or offenders fairly and firmly;

and that it should do so efficiently and effectively.

Collective aims expressed in terms such as these are of quite recent origin. They began to appear in the Home Office Review of Criminal Justice Policy published in 1977, and in the two Home Office "Working Papers" published in the early 1980s (Home Office 1977; 1984). The latest expression is in the White Paper *Protecting the Public* (Home Office 1996a). Before that, during the "liberal consensus" of the 1950s and 1960s, aims were defined in very general terms, and for the most part only for individual services. Those for the police relied on the original guidelines drawn up in 1829 by Sir Richard Mayne and Colonel Rowan, already quoted in Chapter I. For the Prison Service, the aim or purpose was the aspiration set out in Rule 1 of the Prison Rules, which in its present form reads:

> *The purpose of the training and treatment of convicted prisoners shall be to encourage and assist them to lead a good and useful life.*

For the Probation Service it was to *advise, assist and befriend offenders* in accordance with the Probation of Offenders Act 1907. For the courts it was the judicial oath:

> *.... to do right to all manner of people after the laws and usages of this realm, without fear, favour, affection or ill-will.*

13

Successive governments of that period saw themselves as responsible for the framework of law, administrative structure and finance within which the courts and the operational services could carry out their various functions to suitable standards and subject to suitable safeguards. Particular tasks were set by the services themselves, and often by individuals within them, with relatively little direction from central government. Ministers did not yet see themselves as managing a system, or as setting objectives which the services were expected to achieve on their behalf.

1970s: Impetus for Change

The 1970s were a difficult period. They saw rising crime; dissention within the police, leading to the Edmund Davies inquiry into police pay; dissatisfaction with the structure of higher courts, resulting in the Beeching reforms and the creation of the Crown Court under the Courts Act 1971; disturbances and industrial action in prisons, leading to the May Inquiry (Home Office 1979); and disillusion with the effectiveness of sentencing and the treatment of offenders - the attitude that "nothing works", overstated and misunderstood though it may have been (Martinson 1974; 1979; Brody 1975; Hood 1995). New issues were coming into prominence - racial discrimination and harassment, the long-standing neglect of victims, the scope for preventive measures separate from the processes of criminal investigation and law enforcement. Practices such as the censorship of prisoners' letters and the conduct of prison adjudications were being successfully challenged in the European Court of Human Rights (Richardson 1985; 1993; Fawcett 1985; Morgan 1994).

All these developments challenged existing policies and traditional attitudes and assumptions. They required a degree of co-operation and mutual understanding between services, courts and voluntary agencies which had not been contemplated before. It was time for more decisive action and leadership, by government and by the courts and the services themselves. As already stated in Chapter III, new insights into the nature and extent of crime and the characteristics of criminality became available from the British Crime Survey and the Offenders Index.

1980s: A New Sense of Direction

Events began to take a new direction from about 1980 onwards. While disturbances and industrial action continued to take place in prisons; while the police were facing accusations of malpractice in the Confait investigation and disorder on the streets of Brixton, Toxteth and other places, both the Government and the services themselves were trying to develop a stronger sense of purpose, coherence and principle. The Government was to a large extent driven by the Thatcher administration's Financial Management Initiative and its demands for efficiency, economy and effectiveness; the services - and to some extent the Government itself - were at the same time responding to the changing social, political and economic environment. It is easy to think of the change of Government in 1979 as a turning point, but many of the subsequent changes were built on ideas which had been developed some time previously. The Criminal Justice Acts of 1982 and 1988, for example, built on proposals for the custodial sentencing and treatment of young adults which the Advisory Council on the Penal System had put forward in 1974 (Advisory Council on the Penal System 1974; May 1974; Gelsthorpe and Morris 1994).

A central feature of the Government's approach to all public policy during the 1980s was its insistence on financial information and analysis; on setting targets and objectives; and on measuring results and outcomes. New statements of purpose were issued for the police, prison and probation services. For the police it was:

The purpose of the police service is to uphold the law fairly and firmly; to prevent crime; to pursue and bring to justice those who break the law; to keep The Queen's peace; to protect, help and reassure the community; and to be seen to do this with integrity, common-sense and sound judgment.

For the Prison Service:

Her Majesty's Prison Service serves the public by keeping in custody those committed by the courts.

Our duty is to look after them with humanity, and to help them to lead law-abiding and useful lives, in custody and after release.

And, for the Probation Service:

The Probation Service serves the courts and the public by:
- *supervising offenders in the community;*
- *helping offenders to lead law-abiding lives;*
- *safeguarding the welfare of children and family proceedings.*
The Probation Service operates locally under area probation committees or boards within a framework of national standards.

There was some disappointment that the material available from research and statistics give inconclusive answers to questions about the causes of crime or the means of preventing re-offending, but there was enough to show that attempts to reduce crime cannot rely exclusively on the processes of detection, prosecution, conviction and sentence. There were serious questions about the effectiveness of some aspects of policing, especially patrol (Clarke and Hough 1984; Audit Commission 1996); and it was recognised that an indefinite expansion of prison accommodation, or of the prison population, does not provide value for money in terms of its effect on the general level of crime or on the subsequent behaviour of individual offenders (Home Office 1990).

Into the 1990s

The result was the development of a set of policies which reflected the aims indicated at the beginning of this chapter. They could be seen as having as more specific objectives to:

- prevent and reduce crime;
- establish a more coherent and principled basis for sentencing and parole;
- avoid the unnecessary use of imprisonment and stabilise the prison population;
- develop schemes of supervision in the community which would effectively reduce re-offending;
- give greater consideration to victims; and
- make the system more efficient, effective and accountable (Windlesham 1993, Faulkner 1995a; Rutherford 1996).

The principles underlying these objectives included proportionality in sentencing; structured decision-making; due process and accountability in administration, including recognised and accessible channels for complaint; equity in the provision of services; and respect for individuals, including those who are members of ethnic or cultural minorities.

Ambiguity and Uncertainty

It was difficult for Ministers to express these objectives, and still more these principles, in a straightforward, unambiguous way when it was at the same time politically necessary to give an over-riding impression of being "tough on crime". One consequence was the "twin track" or "bifurcatory" approach to sentencing which came to be embodied in the Criminal Justice Act 1991 (Cavadino and Dignan 1992). This approach promoted community sentences for minor offenders and longer prison sentences for serious, and especially violent and sexual, offenders, but with the public emphasis always on the latter. Another was the rhetoric of "punishment in the community", with its emphasis on the demanding nature of the requirements imposed by probation and community service orders to the exclusion of their rehabilitative or preventive effect (admittedly difficult to demonstrate in any event) (Home Office 1988; 1990). A third, which was also consistent with the traditions of English legislative drafting, was the absence from legislation of any statutory sentencing principles, as distinct from procedural requirements, to reinforce the provisions on sentencing in successive criminal justice acts, and especially the Act of 1991 (Lacey 1994b). The resulting ambiguity made it easier for the courts to interpret the legislation in their own terms, and for the Government itself to abandon its earlier objectives when it became politically convenient to do so.

A Change of Course

A change of political mood took place at about the end of 1992, followed by a dramatic change in the Government's own political direction. It was partly a response to genuine public concern, shared by the police and the courts, about the continued rise in crime. But its origin can also be traced to the internal difficulties of the Conservative Party at the time of the collapse of the Exchange Rate Mechanism and the Maastricht Treaty. However that may be, the change was for the most part supported by the other political parties. It was accompanied by intensive, sensational and often ill-informed reporting in the media.

During the two years 1992-1993, the police conducted a sophisticated and mostly successful campaign for more punitive action to be taken against persistent juvenile offenders, and later for changes in the law on the right of silence and on disclosure of evidence. Both campaigns were based on uncertain evidence - facts asserted confidently by the police but with little systematic empirical data. The judiciary resented the perceived interference with their discretion contained in the Criminal Justice Act 1991 and sought to resist it politically, in pressing for the Act's amendment, and to re-interpret its provisions, for example, through judgments in the Court of Appeal (Taylor 1993; Ashworth 1995a). The prison population started to rise as courts responded to the new political climate, taking advantage of the flexibility and sometimes the ambiguity of the Act despite their earlier criticism of the rigidity which they claimed it imposed.

In response to these pressures, the Government introduced, in the Criminal Justice Act 1993, a range of provisions to amend the sentencing provisions of the 1991 Act, and effectively abandoned its earlier attempts to restrain the growth in the prison population and to promote the use of community sentences as the normal disposal for all but the most serious offences. Crime prevention receded from the political agenda, and no action was taken on the principal recommendations of the Home Office Standing Conference on Crime Prevention in its important and widely welcomed report on *Safer Communities: The Local Delivery of Crime Prevention through the Partnership Approach* - the Morgan Report (Home Office 1991b). The aims of the police set out in the White Paper on Police Reform concentrated on law enforcement and the detection and arrest of criminals, and made no mention of the preventive role and public service role which had featured prominently in the statement of purpose three years before (Home Office 1993; ACPO 1990). Issues relating to victims became dominated by controversy over the Government's proposals for reforming the Criminal Injuries Compensation Scheme in order to control its costs, and the eventual passage of the Criminal Injuries Compensation Act 1995.

At the same time, the practical managerialism of the early 1980s was giving way to a more assertive and more dogmatic form of central direction, across the whole of government, based on notions of contracts and markets. Power was increasingly concentrated at the centre; and responsibility, and blame when things went wrong, was devolved to local managers. A new commercial model was being superimposed upon the professional, bureaucratic and (in the police and prison services) command structures which had competed with one another in the past (Freedland 1994; Jenkins 1995; Police Federation/Policy Studies Institute 1996).

Standards for the treatment of prisoners had originally been conceived, for example by the United Nations and the Council of Europe, as an instrument of penal reform (Fawcett 1985): standards, or "key performance indicators", came to be applied - in prisons and elsewhere - as an instrument of standardisation, audit, risk avoidance and government control (King and McDermott 1995). Combined with the emphasis on punishment, intended in the 1980s to give credibility to community sentences, the new form of political managerialism began to substitute a culture of mechanical enforcement and compliance for the ideas personal progress and development, or rehabilitation, which had traditionally informed probation programmes and prison regimes (Hudson 1987, May 1994). The Government's development of probation service standards, its proposals on probation training, and its consultation paper on *Strengthening Punishment in the Community* are obvious examples (Home Office 1994; 1995e).

An Instrumental View of Justice

Alongside this development, the Government began to assert, and impose, an instrumental view of justice which saw the process of prosecution, conviction and sentence not as a means of achieving for its own sake but as an instrument of social control. This instrumental view is reflected, for example, in the terms of reference and eventual report of the Royal Commission on Criminal Justice (Royal Commission on Criminal Justice 1993) - set up as a response to dramatic miscarriages of justice, but as much concerned in the outcome to increase the total number of convictions as to reduce the number which might be wrongful or unsafe (Lacey 1994b; Sanders 1994a; Ashworth 1996). The language was far removed from Blackstone's dictum that *it is better that ten guilty persons escape than one innocent suffers* (Blackstone 1765).

The instrumental view is also reflected in the White Paper on Police Reform (Home Office 1993), with its emphasis on law enforcement and the detection of criminals as the principal functions of the police; and its neglect of those functions which are concerned with preventing crime, protecting the weak and vulnerable, and solving problems of social disorder. The White Paper, and the Police and Magistrates' Courts Bill which followed, were accompanied by political and media campaigns to reinforce the culture of aggressive law enforcement and to discredit the ideas of public accountability, responsiveness and community policing which the police themselves had successfully developed following the Scarman report on the urban disorders at the beginning of the 1980s and the Police and Criminal Evidence Act 1984 (Hill 1994; Reiner 1994). A similarly instrumental view of education, for example, would see its purpose as being not to create an informed, intelligent and cultured society, but to train an efficient workforce so that British industry and commerce could compete successfully in international markets.

The most recent White Paper *Protecting the Public* (Home Office 1996a) shows a further significant change in the Government's position. Interestingly, in relation to the police, it once again recognises the importance of their preventive role, and the public trust and local consultation, as well as emphasising the importance of efficiency and effectiveness in controlling crime. In relation to the courts, it restates the Government's (or more accurately Parliament's) traditional role in providing a statutory framework for sentencing; but it breaks entirely new ground, in modern times, in proposing a framework which in important respects eliminates the court's discretion to impose the sentence which it considers to be just in the particular case before it. The argument is based entirely on the supposed protection for the public, to the exclusion of any sense of justice for the individual (see also Chapter VIII below).

Conclusions which can be drawn from the events of the last 15 years include the following:

- Governments, leaders of the criminal justice services and the courts must take an active role in providing a sense of purpose and direction; in managing the services and institutions which make up the criminal justice system; and in co-ordinating the work of the system as a whole.

- Policies, legislation and administrative measures for tackling crime have to be planned, implemented and tested as part of a co-ordinated strategic approach based on information, analysis, consultation and judgment.

- They need to have clearly defined, realistic purposes, and to be based on clearly stated principles reflecting an "inclusive" rather than an "exclusive" view of society and criminal justice.

- Services and the courts need to be clearly accountable locally as well as nationally.

- Suitable structures are needed to support this process.

Chapters VIII-X discuss how these conclusions might be applied in practice.

CHAPTER V

Children and Young People

Legal and Historical Background

The criminal law made no distinction between children and adults until well into the nineteenth century, and children were hanged or transported with a brutality that was mitigated only by the law's haphazard enforcement. Recognition that children deserved a separate status, and respect for their own identity and interests, featured in the work of the Victorian reformers and was carried into statute, for example, in the Children and Young Persons Acts of 1933 and 1969, and the Children Act 1989. But arguments continue, for instance, over the extent to which the parents can be expected, or entitled, to control their children's actions, and who is then to be held responsible for them. Instances can be found in relation to binding over, the payment of fines or compensation, enforcing attendance at school, access to contraceptive advice or the use of corporal punishment. Other issues concern the age of majority, the ages at which young people should be permitted by law to buy alcohol or tobacco, to drive cars or consent to sexual intercourse. Many of these issues have been familiar for a long time, but recent developments have included the divisional court's decision, subsequently reversed on appeal, to abandon the principle of *doli incapax* - the requirement that a child under 14 should know that the act was wrong before being convicted of a criminal offence; and the provision in the Sexual Offences Act 1993 which lowered the age at which a person can be held capable of the offence of rape.

The tension has traditionally been between a "welfare" approach to juvenile justice in which courts and social workers are expected to know what is in the child's best interests and act accordingly; and a "justice" approach by which children are expected to take responsibility for their actions and if necessary to be punished for them, but with the protection of the criminal justice process (Morris and Giller 1987). Recent developments, including the demonising of children and the "exclusive" view of society mentioned in previous chapters, have reinforced the "justice" approach and have added a punitive element to it. Results can be seen in the increased penalties for children and young persons and the provisions for secure training orders for children aged 12-14 contained in the Criminal Justice and Public Order Act 1994; and the substantial increase in the numbers of children and young people detained in prison establishments, both under sentence and on remand (Howard League 1995a; 1995c; Cervi 1996). Few other European countries give so little protection to children under their criminal law - the age of criminal responsibility in most countries is between 14 and 16 - and the United

Kingdom has been criticised for failing to observe the requirements of the United Nations Convention on the Rights of the Child (Howard League 1995c; JUSTICE 1996).

Social and Economic Background

These are difficult and turbulent times for young people, and especially for young men (Rutter and Smith 1995). Many of the landmarks and signposts which were available to guide earlier generations have been removed. The prospects of stable employment are much less than they were twenty years ago and life time careers can no longer be expected. The chances of obtaining employment are often better for women than for men (although much of it is short-term, part-time and low-paid), which with other changes in the position and expectations of women affects relationships between men and women and perhaps makes them harder to sustain. Satisfactory male role models are harder to find. The support, and the dignity and respect, which men gained from working in old industries has disappeared. So has the security which was once assumed in traditional middle class careers.

Fear of crime adds to this pervasive sense of insecurity and leads to a pre-occupation with protection and safety in all aspects of life. It leads to children being driven to school instead of walking or using public transport, and to children being denied the opportunities for discovery and adventure which were taken for granted forty years ago. The fear - or sense of responsibility - which produces this result has to be respected, but the consequences, for children's health and for their sense of confidence, self-reliance and independence, may prove to be damaging (Chunn 1996).

There is clear evidence (Farrington 1994; Graham and Bowling 1995) that offending is commonly associated with:

- low family income;
- poor housing;
- an unstable job record (the offender's or his parents);
- failure or exclusion from school;
- delinquent family or friends;
- a remote father (not necessarily an absent father);
- harsh and erratic discipline (at home or at school);
- abuse of drugs;
- mental disturbance; and
- previous experience of violence or abuse.

Teaching Children Right from Wrong

A lot is said about teaching children right from wrong, or discipline, or respect or authority. It is often suggested that this should be done by restricting what children are allowed to do; by punishment, often physical punishment; and by fear. It is a sad and barren approach for children who are probably living very restricted and poverty stricken lives already and it shows a confused understanding of what punishment should be for and what it can be expected to achieve. Much has been written on that subject, but for this purpose it may be enough to say that children are not taught right from wrong by being put down and humiliated. Nor will much progress be made by telling them that stealing, bullying and telling lies are wrong; and that doing as they are told, working hard at school and being polite to other people are right. To say this is not to argue for "moral relativism": it is simply to recognise that children have to learn to cope with situations, influences and conflicts which cannot be resolved in simple terms, in ways which they can see make sense for them. They need parents and other adults who will listen and understand, who will explain and set an example, who will have time to do all these things, and whom they respect. They need other children with whom to share the experience. And they need to develop a sense of the boundaries of acceptable behaviour, and a set of guiding principles with which to shape their lives (Faulkner 1995b; Leach 1994).

Parents undoubtedly have a crucial role and a special responsibility. Recent legislation, for example the Criminal Justice Act 1991, has sought to reinforce responsibility both for the parents and for their children themselves, but it has usually done so by attempting to penalise parents for their children's behaviour with potentially unjust or damaging consequences. Far less attention has been given to providing support, especially in the important early years (Howard League 1993a; Penal Affairs Consortium 1995d).

Respect for the Law

The criminal law and the criminal justice process have an undoubted part to play in preventing criminality. But it is only one of the many influences which will be at work. Children need to grow up with the knowledge that society, or the state, fixes its own boundaries and is prepared to enforce them. They need to respect those boundaries and the process of enforcement, and to believe that the forces of the state stand ultimately for fairness and justice. They will not have that respect if they see that the law is widely disregarded, whether by their contemporaries or by those in positions of authority; or if they perceive it to be arbitrarily, capriciously or oppressively enforced. But just as important - perhaps more important - than respect for the law is their own sense of duty and responsibility. That has to be learned from the example of others and they are entitled to expect it from others in return.

Persistent Juvenile Offenders

There is a lot of debate about the extent to which there is amongst young people a hard core of persistent juvenile offenders who are responsible for a disproportionate amount of crime in particular areas and at particular times (Hagell and Newburn 1994; Graham and Bowling 1995). Newspapers will report cases where a young man has committed, or is suspected of committing, offences which may run into hundreds; and the police will sometimes claim that if the known persistent offenders were removed from circulation, the level of crime in the area would significantly decrease. These claims are the reason for the secure training centres and secure training orders to be introduced under the Criminal Justice and Public Order Act 1994 (Howard League 1995a). The persistent juvenile offender becomes much harder to identify when the task is to create a system for dealing with him (or occasionally her). It is not clear how many persistent offenders there are, and different definitions will identify different individuals (Hagell and Newburn 1994). Individuals identified today will probably not be the same as those identified three months ago or in three months' time. It is still less clear if they can be identified in advance, or if they could, what could be done with them. They cannot justly be punished for what they have not yet done, or given privileges which are not available to others who may be thought equally or more deserving. Many young people will share similar characteristics but not become offenders. What will usually be true is that most persistent offenders will have chaotic and often tragic lives; parents and schools will have had little influence; and they will have reached a point where notions of honesty, decency or consideration for others take second place to day to day survival - not in terms of life or death, but of managing and coping in a complex, difficult and, as it often seems to them, hostile world (Graef 1992; Utting et al 1993; Holman 1995).

Children and Mental Health

Severe mental illness affects 250,000 children in the UK or about two percent of children under the age of 16. Two million children suffer from mental ill-health, half of whom have moderate to severe problems. Suicides increased by about 45% in 15 to 19 year old young men between the late 1970s and the late 1980s. Even amongst three year olds, moderate to severe behaviour problems are present in seven percent of those in the inner cities, with another 15 percent having less serious difficulties. The risk of childhood mental illness increases in families where parents are unemployed, divorced, living alone or homeless, where the mother suffers depression, or where child abuse occurs. Adult mental illness, particularly depression, is linked to similar factors in childhood: damage done in early life may have a serious lasting effect (Kurtz et al 1994; Mental Health Foundation 1995; Department of Health/Department for Education 1995; Wallace et al 1995; Health Advisory Service 1995).

Children with mental health problems may be seen and treated in widely different ways by the people and agencies involved. Schools may see such children as slow learners, dis-

23

affected or troublesome, with responses ranging from special classes to exclusion. Juvenile justice agencies may see them as "delinquent" and adopt increasingly punitive approaches. Social services may identify family problems and consider Children Act orders. Health professionals frequently fail to recognise mental health problems in young people, and are overstretched and often poorly organised; too often, children end up in adult wards and other inappropriate settings. Parents' own concerns may be compounded by the confusion of approaches from professionals.

The lack of any coherent or integrated approach by professional agencies reflects a broader crisis of confidence in society's view of childhood and of parenting. Social changes have increased expectations of parents while reducing the supports traditionally available to them. Extended family networks have been eroded; far fewer families have one parent at home rather than at work; there has been a reduction in the pastoral role of professionals such as teachers; and more people live in poverty.

The mental health of children has risen rapidly up the priorities of many agencies. This rise is reflected in current and recent work by the Health Advisory Service, Audit Commission, Department of Health and others. These programmes of work are valuable, but a broader view must also be taken. Education, juvenile justice and social services all play a vital part in affecting the mental health of children and young people, as do broader social welfare issues such as benefits, employment and housing.

A Programme to Reduce Criminality

A comprehensive programme is now needed to reduce criminality among young people. It should focus on children's experiences in childhood, and the means by which they learn to respect the feelings and property of others. It should provide guidance and practical support for parents, especially isolated parents, in dealing with difficult and challenging behaviour. Arrangements for pre-school education should be an important element. Within schools it should involve teaching about relationships, the prevention of bullying and the identification and support for children at risk (Devlin 1995). Exclusion from school should be avoided wherever possible, and alternative provision for education and discipline should be made if exclusion becomes inevitable. Local partnerships should be established, involving schools, the youth service, and social services. They must be accessible to parents, children and their extended families from all social, ethnic and cultural backgrounds (Home Office 1996a; Leff 1996).

The programme should include a systematic and comprehensive review of the arrangements for care, homes and institutions for those who for whatever reason cannot remain with their own families in their own homes. The structure of these arrangements is at present confused, with no consistent pattern between different parts of the country. The arrangements to be made in particular cases depend as much on what is locally available and the state of the local authority's budget, as on the situation and needs of difficult children themselves, or of their families and communities. The proposed secure training centres will add to the confusion, especially when the attraction of central funding will provide an incentive for report writers to recommend their use in preference to local authorities' own accommodation. Some extra secure provision is certainly needed, but it needs a much more coherent structure of standards and accountability and more systematic integration with services in the community.

The programme must also pay attention to the opportunities and temptations for young people in making their transition to adult life, before and after leaving school. An especially important group are those exceptionally vulnerable young people leaving local authority care. The objective must be to provide a sense of hope and progress, where possible, through further education, training and a realistic prospect of employment, but also through structured and challenging activities which can provide their own sense of achievement and reward.

Successful programmes for working with young people are likely to have the following characteristics (Barrett and Greenaway 1995; Huskins forthcoming):

- a clear and convincing rationale for what they will achieve and how they will work;

- a precise focus on the types of behaviour to be addressed and the groups of young people to be involved, with a clear understanding of their social environment and any differences of gender and culture;

- a well planned progression through different levels of experience, responsibility and understanding, with lessons learnt and interpreted at each stage;

- effective procedures for assessment and review, including self-assessment by young people themselves; and

- links between the activities in the programme and young people's home environment, with long term understanding and support from the local communities concerned.

There is a special challenge for outreach youth work; and there may be special opportunities for outdoor adventure and voluntary service provided that there is a clear sense of purpose and an orderly and disciplined approach.

These are the issues which the new Ministerial Group on Juveniles, announced in the recent White Paper (Home Office 1996a) should pay urgent attention.

CHAPTER VI

Preventing and Reducing Crime

Earlier chapters have referred to the widespread belief, reinforced by the political and media campaigns of the last three years, that crime can be dealt with by relying almost entirely on the criminal justice system - the procedures of detection, arrest, prosecution, conviction and punishment. From this viewpoint, the way to stop crime is to catch more criminals, see that more of them are convicted, send more of them to prison, and treat them more harshly when they get there. This belief may seem logical to those who have settled lives and living conditions, who are used to making rational choices and have the opportunity to do so, and who have something to lose - status, position and the respect of others.

Rigorous enforcement or severe sentencing may be effective when they are associated with social pressures, for example, against drinking and driving, and may have contributed to the improvement in road safety which has taken place over the last twenty years. They may succeed in displacing organised crime. Crime would certainly increase if all efforts to enforce the criminal law were abandoned, or if they were perceived to be wholly ineffective. But it is unrealistic to suppose that law enforcement or sentencing on their own will influence behaviour in ways which would have a significant effect on the general level of crime (Cornish and Clarke 1986; Police Foundation/Policy Studies Institute 1996). Those who desist from persistent offending will usually do so gradually and over a period of time (Burnett 1994a; 1994b; Graham and Bowling 1995).

Chapter I referred to the evidence that only a small proportion of the crime uncovered by the British Crime Survey is brought to a caution or a conviction in court - about three per cent. Less than one per cent results in a custodial sentence. Measures to target, deter or detect known or potential offenders may have some deterrent effect on the level of some offences in some areas, and prison sentences will have some incapacitating effect in preventing offenders from committing offences against the public during the period of their imprisonment. Their value, for some offences and in some situations, should certainly not be discounted. But they do not provide the basis for a comprehensive programme to tackle the problem of crime. Part of the effect may be to displace crime to other areas or other types of offence; and targeted policing, even if resources are available to support it, can have a price in terms of community relations and public support (Reiner 1994; Police Foundation/Policy Studies Institute 1996). The deterrent results to be achieved by increasing levels of punishment are even more questionable (Baxter and Nuttall 1975; Brody 1975; Hood 1989).

As for the incapacitating effect of imprisonment, Home Office studies indicate that there would have to be a very substantial increase in the prison population before it could have a perceptible effect on the level of actual crime (Tarling 1993).

The conclusion must be - as the police have regularly claimed and as the Government has recognised in its White Paper, *Protecting the Public* - that measures to prevent and reduce crime cannot be sought only through the criminal justice system and the criminal justice process (Heal 1991; Home Office 1996a).

Crime Prevention

Programmes to prevent crime and reduce criminality have been of broadly two kinds. One consists of measures designed to make crime harder to commit or easier to detect, typically by improving security or observation. The other attempts to influence the potential offender's motivation. The former are a good deal more straightforward, conceptually and operationally, than the latter. They are also easier to justify and evaluate in terms of quantified results. They include stronger or more sophisticated security for buildings, vehicles and premises, improved lighting, changes in the design and construction of housing estates or shopping areas, the use of security guards and schemes such as Neighbourhood Watch. Those intended to make it easier to detect include the installation of closed circuit television, DNA testing and - it has been suggested - the carrying of identity cards.

Programmes for reducing criminality raise wider and more difficult issues. The early identification of people thought to be "at risk", followed by special attention to encourage their successful development, or alternatively to subject them to various forms of control, involves questions both of practicability and of natural justice. Accurate identification is difficult, and special attention is likely to be given to large numbers of people who would progress successfully without it, or alternatively to miss many of those for whom it is intended. It is also likely to be seen as unfair - as rewarding those who do not deserve it if it is favourable, or as discriminatory and stigmatising if it is not. A more promising approach, so far as children are concerned, has been described in the previous chapter. Similar objections can be made to schemes for encouraging older offenders or people at risk, for example by giving them opportunities for training or employment, or to develop new interests. Further difficulties arise when programmes to reduce criminality start to raise wider issues of social values; poverty, inequality, the role of the family or of schools; and of social policies in such areas as employment, social security, housing and education.

However that may be, there is increasing evidence that schemes to prevent crime by physical means are likely to have limited success unless they are backed up by schemes to reduce criminality (Nelken 1995; Osborn and Shaftoe 1995). Some of them may reflect a defensive outlook and the "exclusive" attitude described in Chapter II, and part

27

of their effect could be to provoke feelings of rejection and alienation which could themselves lead to crime. Although the effect of social and economic conditions on individual behaviour, or on the general level of crime, are difficult to measure or predict, they cannot be ignored (Field 1990; Graham and Bowling 1995). One of the most complete accounts of the links between crime and the wider issues of social policy, training, education, employment, social security and housing is in the report of NACRO's Committee on Crime and Social Policy (NACRO 1995). In each of these areas, the report made important recommendations; on crime and responsibility; on the labour market and crime; on the family and crime; and on neighbourhoods and crime, all of which deserve serious attention.

Organisation and Structure

Since crime prevention became a focus of serious attention in the early 1980s, responsibility at local level has been awkwardly divided between local government and the police. Both have often seen it as a matter of marginal importance, and the resources devoted to preventive work have always been trivial in relation to expenditure on other programmes (it represents only about two per cent of total spending on criminal justice) (Loveday 1994; Police Foundation/Policy Studies Institute 1996).

Mention has already been made of the important review of crime prevention policies which was carried out by an independent working group of the Home Office Standing Conference on Crime Prevention, under the chairmanship of James Morgan. Its report (Home Office 1991b) was warmly welcomed by local authorities, the police and others. It has stimulated several initiatives at local level. But it received a half-hearted response from central government, and in particular no action has been taken on one of its central recommendations, that ... *local authorities, working in conjunction with the police, should have clear statutory responsibility for the development and stimulation of community safety and crime prevention programmes, and for progressing at local level a multi-agency approach to community safety.*

Stimulated by the Morgan Report and by local influences in their own areas, many local authorities, police forces, probation services, social services departments and voluntary organisations have formed partnerships to promote community safety and reduce crime. Some have formed new charitable organisations for this purpose, with full time staff (for example the Thames Valley Partnership); others have worked in less structured ways. Some have had the benefit of guidance from organisations like Crime Concern, NACRO or the Divert Trust, or of funding from central government through the Single Regeneration Budget or the Safer Cities or other programmes; others have worked independently. Some have attempted a comprehensive approach; others have concentrated on particular aspects or groups at risk. All have found enthusiasm and good will. All have found that joint working requires changes of outlook and attitude, including a readiness to share information and influence, among both managers and first line staff. All have found difficulty with funding, and especially with the bureaucracy involved in obtaining funds from central government. All have found it difficult to make the transition from short term, specially funded, self contained - and therefore vulnerable - projects to permanent schemes and ultimately to new methods of work which form a natural part of each service's ordinary programme. The techniques can be difficult and laborious and the outcomes are often inconclusive. There is in most areas a strong commitment to continuing the process of change and to developing the techniques of evaluation, but it needs to be sustained by consistent support at professional, managerial and political levels.

The Way Ahead

Measures to reduce crime and criminality must be founded on broadly based programmes at local and national levels. Such programmes must aim to create and sustain effective partnerships between statutory and voluntary organisations, businesses and individuals; and to generate stronger, more confident and more inclusive communities. They must be supported by central government, through policies which are co-ordinated between departments and informed by consultation and research. Programmes must include measures which aim both to make crime harder to commit and easier to detect, and to influence the motivation of offenders and potential offenders and the temptations and opportunities which are available to them. Funding must not be accompanied by bureaucratic requirements - imposed, for example, to generate competition - which effectively deter smaller organisations from taking part.

Specific measures should include:

- programmes for children, young people and parents as indicated in Chapter V;

- implementation of the Morgan Report, including its recommendation for a statutory duty upon local authorities;

- independent audit to assess the impact on crime and criminality of current and proposed social and economic policies;

- targets and key performance indicators for statutory services and for government funded regeneration schemes, to include reductions in crime;

- flexible arrangements for commissioning and purchasing, including joint funding, to encourage initiative and innovation, without imposing a burdensome bureaucracy;

- a shift of resources from punishment (especially imprisonment) to prevention; and

- arrangements to generate a spirit of shared commitment and responsibility, based on a sense of public service and obligation and common citizenship.

These are matters for the attention of the National Crime Prevention Agency and the Ministerial Group on Crime Prevention, but effective action can only take place at a local level.

CHAPTER VII

Reducing the Damage

Policies to reduce the damage caused by crime focus to a large extent on the victim. A great deal has been achieved for victims in recent years, but the extent of that achievement is itself raising questions about the nature of victims' legitimate expectations from the state, from the criminal justice system and from society more generally; and about the means, and cost, of satisfying those expectations.

What has been Achieved

Compensation for the victims of violent crime has been available for over thirty years, but the Criminal Injuries Compensation Scheme has been progressively, and restrictively, modified during that period. It has also come under increasing criticism for the extent to which some victims are effectively excluded from its scope. The Government itself concluded that the scheme could no longer be afforded in its earlier form and published plans for a new and more restricted scheme (Home Office 1993b). Its attempts to put the new and more restricted scheme into effect by administrative action were successfully challenged in the courts, but legislation for a new scheme has now been enacted by Parliament.

More significant for most victims, including the vast majority who suffer not from physical violence but from crimes against their homes or property, has been the establishment and expansion of victim support schemes throughout the country. They include arrangements to support victims and witnesses when they attend court. These changes have come about largely through the efforts of Victim Support and other, more specialised, voluntary bodies. This development has been accompanied by a greater awareness of victims' issues, and a greater sensitivity to their feelings and situations, in all the relevant statutory services. A statement of what victims are entitled to expect was set out in the Victim's Charter - the forerunner of the Citizen's Charter - in 1990.

Current Concerns

There is still, however, concern that many of those expectations are not being met in practice, and that other needs are scarcely being addressed at all. The most recent initiatives, such as the requirement for pre-sentence reports to include a reference to the impact on the victim, and the "help line" to enable victims to express opinions about the arrangements for a prisoner's release or home leave, have been criticised as hasty and not fully thought out. More radical suggestions are being made that victims should have a right to make a statement to the court describing their feelings and reactions; and that by this means or otherwise they should be able to express views on matters such as bail, the choice of charge, the granting of bail, the acceptance of a plea, and the sentence (Mills B 1995).

Any discussion of the position of victims has to recognise:

- the acute sense of frustration, exploitation and sometimes humiliation and betrayal which many victims feel about the way in which they are treated at present;

- the fact that victims and offenders are not separate groups of people: that they are often members of the same communities, and that (as already stated) many victims have previously been offenders and vice versa;

- the genuine limitations of what is feasible and affordable in providing for compensation, whether by the state or by offenders, or in according "rights" to victims in an adversarial system of justice where the parties are the offender and the state.

The issues to be considered are broadly of three kinds: the arrangements for compensation; the services (information, facilities, advice, support) to which victims should be entitled, and the means of providing them; and the position of the victim in the criminal justice process, especially in respect of decisions relating to the suspect or offender.

Compensation

Arguments on compensation have focused largely on the Government's proposals to replace the previous Criminal Injuries Compensation Scheme, based on individual assessment and common law damages, with a "tariff" scheme based on fixed, and for some victims less favourable, rates of award. The arguments concentrated largely on the legality of the new proposals, to the exclusion of more general considerations and principles. The effect has been to neglect some of the wider issues, including those identified in the review of compensation carried out by an independent working party set up by Victim Support (Victim Support 1993). That report considered the principles which should govern the provision of compensation for victims of crime, the purposes which it should attempt to achieve, and the relationship between compensation for the effects of crime and other forms of state benefit, together with the obligations which could be expected from employers and other organisations such as insurance companies. It drew attention to a number of criticisms of the original scheme, few of which have been met in the new arrangements. Examples are the exclusion of all offences against property and of injuries where the claim is assessed at less than £1,000; the loss, in many cases, of social security benefits; the disqualification for previous, unrelated criminal offences; and the treatment of the families of victims of homicide. The report recommended some immediate changes, and a longer term programme of development which it recognised might need to extend over a period of several years. With the legislation for the new compensation scheme now in place, these questions should now be addressed, with particular attention to the criticisms indicated earlier in this paragraph.

Services for Victims

Services for victims are relatively straightforward, in the sense that there is no serious dispute about the need for the services themselves. Victims need information, practical and emotional support; they may need counselling or medical treatment and sometimes physical protection; they always need recognition and to be treated with dignity and respect. The main questions are about how services should be delivered in practice; the responsibilities of the relevant statutory and voluntary agencies; the means (if any) by which those responsibilities could be enforced by or in behalf of the victim; and, inevitably, the resource implications. These questions are being considered in a review which the Government has undertaken in the Victim's Charter (Home Office 1996a). The objectives should be a statement of victims' legitimate expectations which are comprehensive, clear and decisive; and the introduction of suitable machinery and procedures to ensure that they are effectively met.

A revision of the Victim's Charter is, however, only the starting point. The critical issue, for services to victims and for public services generally, is the quality and dynamics of the relationships through which they are delivered (Burnside and Baker 1994). Relationships can be affected by the culture and morale of the service concerned, the commitment of its managers, and the degree of confidence and genuine communication between service providers and victims and among service providers themselves. They can be damaged by conflict or lack of clarity in the service's objectives, or by lack of will at management or operational level. Change can be brought about by setting standards and monitoring performance in the way that is likely to be proposed, but the standards themselves should be of a kind which promote confidence and satisfaction in relationships with victims and not simply speed or volume of service. They must focus on "external" outcomes as well as "internal" processes and outputs.

There may also be a case for developing a formal procedure for complaints. There are dangers in encouraging a culture of criticism and complaint, but such a procedure could bring benefits if, like the new procedure for complaints in the health service, it is designed to operate in a spirit of conciliation rather than confrontation. Another possibility would be the designation of readily accessible liaison officers, or liaison teams, in each of the relevant statutory services; or of jointly appointed liaison officers who would function on behalf of the criminal justice service as a whole. All these possibilities should be seriously considered.

More radical proposals would involve imposing statutory duties on the services and conferring justiciable rights on victims; or giving statutory responsibilities for the care of victims to one of the existing services; creating a new statutory service for this purpose. The former would however involve substantial bureaucracy; its procedures would be laborious and expensive for victims to activate; and it must be questionable whether they would be any more effective than the less formal measures discussed in the previous paragraph. The latter would involve an even greater bureaucracy, and a substantial increase in public expenditure; it would also displace, duplicate or nationalise voluntary organisations such as Victim Support which have successfully established themselves in this area of work.

Mediation and Conciliation

Interest is increasingly being expressed in schemes for involving victims in procedures for mediation or conciliation. Such arrangements bring victims and offenders face-to-face, in the presence of a mediator, with the aim of enabling victims to express their feelings and reactions to the experience they have suffered, and offenders to find some explanation of their own intentions and motivation. Such meetings may take place as an alternative to a prosecution and trial, or as a preliminary or follow up to a criminal trial. In Australia and New Zealand, a "family group conference" - with relatives of both sides often present - is in effect the form of trial which is commonly adopted for young people charged with any but the most serious of offences (Braithwaite 1993). The "Children's Hearing" in Scotland has some similar characteristics (Howard League 1995c).

Schemes of this kind may be promoted with different aims and with different kinds of motivation. Those who promote them will usually claim that they are for the benefit of the victim, but it sometimes appears that the real beneficiary is the offender - either because he or she may then be treated more leniently by the criminal justice system or diverted from it altogether; or because the experience can be turned to social work advantage in the process of addressing the person's offending behaviour.

Other matters of concern include the difficulty of dealing with cases where the person denies the offence; the danger of exploitation or manipulation (of the victim or the offender); the absence, at present, of any machinery for enforcement; problems of achieving consistency in procedure and outcomes; the role (if any) to be played by lawyers in protecting the parties' interests on both sides; and the time and cost likely to be involved.

Interest in mediation and conciliation may also be prompted as much by dissatisfaction with the formal criminal justice process as by confidence in mediation or conciliation for their own sake. Even so, there are considerable attractions in developing mediation and conciliation especially as a means of dealing with cases where the adversarial nature of the ordinary criminal process has particular difficulty in achieving an outcome which is both procedurally just to the defendant, and fair to the victim and to others who may be involved (Burnside and Baker 1994). Examples include many cases involving children; disputes between neighbours; and matters involving trespass.

The scope should be systematically examined, and procedures developed where practicable.

The Victim's Role in the Criminal Justice Process

Much of the debate about victims tends to characterise them as the passive recipients of services - typically services decided for them by others. Such discourse has been criticised as representing victims as "losers". Even the language of "empowerment" can imply the (often condescending or reluctant) conferment of (normally limited) influence or choice by the powerful upon the weak. Many of the procedures associated with the Citizen's Charter, including those provided by the Victim's Charter, can be represented as defining citizens in a narrow sense as consumers of public services, with an emphasis on choice, for example, which often proves in practice to be restricted to what the authorities are prepared to offer and to what the individual can afford to purchase.

Some of those who speak on behalf of victims have been inclined to say that this is how the state and its agencies still perceive victims, and that this attitude is condescending and demeaning. This view may lead to demands for victims to have a stronger voice and a more decisive influence in such matters as the investigation, cautioning, prosecution and sentencing of cases which affect them; or the terms and conditions on which community or custodial sentences should be served, including questions of release from custody. There is no evidence that victims generally would seek to have an influence of this kind, and some research that suggests they would not (Victim Support 1995). Difficult questions would follow about the obligations which would accompany rights to influence the decision-making process, about the safeguards which would need to be provided for defendants and offenders, and about the procedures through which they would be exercised (Ashworth 1993; 1995b; 1996).

The Victim as Citizen

It may be helpful to examine these questions by reference to the concept of the victim as a citizen, and the expectations which citizenship implies for a person who has been a victim of crime. It may seem attractive, at first sight, to think of citizenship as implying rights, and corresponding obligations, to take an active part in proceedings against an offender who has inflicted injury, harm or loss on the person concerned. But it is equally logical to argue that, just as the rights of citizenship do not extend to the unrestricted use of force or to private vengeance, so they should not extend to a direct influence on decisions about the defendant or offender - see for example the Court of Appeal's judgement in <u>Nunn</u> (CA No 95/2176/22). In both instances the state acts on behalf of its citizens collectively, and the individual's rights could reasonably be limited to the compensation and services discussed earlier in this chapter, and to the reasonable and necessary use of force in self defence, to reasonable protection from danger, and to an assurance that the relevant facts are placed before and properly taken into account by the decision-making authority. The victim should not in a civilised society be allowed to take personal vengeance, or be expected to act as an agent of retribution on behalf of the state.

The debate should certainly continue, but the most promising areas for development are the arrangements for compensation, and for information and support, together with the possible scope for new procedures for mediation and conciliation. Proposals designed to give the victim a direct, or even an indirect, influence on the state's decisions affecting the defendant should be approached with very great caution.

CHAPTER VIII

Managing the System

This chapter examines the "management" of the criminal justice system, as a whole and its component parts. As was pointed out in Chapter IV, it is only in quite recent times that the criminal justice "system" has become a focus of attention as such (occasionally in the 1970s, more so in the 1980s), or that it has been seen as a system to be "managed" (Moxon 1985). Attention is still drawn to the "system's" diversity and its lack of central direction, sometimes with a denial that it is a system at all but usually with an implication that it needs more co-ordination and management control. Attempts to "manage" it have sometimes been viewed with suspicion as a threat to the judicial independence of the courts, the operational independence of chief officers of police or probation, and the professional independence of lawyers and the Crown Prosecution Service. But such criticism as there may have been has become increasingly muted in recent years.

The notion of a "system" which has to be "managed" came to prominence as a result of frustration over such matters as access to records; delays in bringing cases to trial; early tensions between the police and the newly-formed Crown Prosecution Service in the processing of criminal cases; and above all the absence of any effective means of aligning the demands of the courts with the capacity of the Prison Service (and to some extent of probation services) to give effect to their sentencing and other decisions. More recent frustrations have been concerned with funding, and with the obstacles to achieving effective co-operation between services at local level. Those obstacles are particularly significant at a time when complex issues have been coming into prominence which can only be dealt with effectively through systematic co-operation between the different services. Some examples - problems relating to children and young people, crime prevention, the treatment of victims - have been discussed in previous chapters.

A different, but politically more serious, source of frustration has been the system's perceived failure to resolve or even engage with more than a small proportion of the total volume of crime that is experienced by ordinary people (Home Office 1995a; Rose 1996). That failure has come to be seen as evidence that crime is becoming "out of control", and that the system is "ineffective". The result is the complex problem of confidence, already discussed in the first chapter, to which the system, and the Government, have to respond. An expression of that frustration can be found in the recent Position Paper by the Association of Chief Police Officers (ACPO 1995).

The new emphasis on management in criminal justice coincided with the acceleration of the Government's reforms of the public service more generally, and the change in outlook and values which accompanied them (see Chapter IV). The most prominent examples are the changes in the structure of the police and the magistrates courts brought about by the Police and Magistrates Courts Act 1994; agency status for the court and prison services; and the contracting out of prison service establishments and functions. Their general intention, and effect, has been to increase the direction and control - especially the political control - of central government; and to devolve accountability (or responsibility - the language is often confusing) to operational management. The drive for greater efficiency has brought important gains in cost effectiveness, but also its own increase in bureaucracy, and a management culture of blaming individuals and of avoiding risk. The new structures create the possibility of tension, and a potential conflict of interest, between the political administration of the day and those responsible for the services' day-to-day management. It is too soon to assess the likely nature or extent of this conflict; or the means by which would be resolved, for example, by litigation. But it is an area of concern, and of potential danger, which needs constant vigilance.

Efficiency and Fairness

It is important to distinguish between efficiency, with its associated qualities of effectiveness and value for money; and fairness with its associated values of equity, accountability and legitimacy. Both are essential components of criminal justice and neither should be sacrificed to the other. Holding the balance between them is, or should be, implicit in maintaining the rule of law.

Efficiency and fairness have been explicit aims of government policy, and of the services themselves, for several years. The emphasis has changed over time to match changing political situations and public expectations and, sometimes, increased understanding and knowledge. During the 1980s efficiency was seen in terms of improved financial information and financial management; clear definition of objectives; and the cost effective use of resources. Intended outcomes included a stable prison population, brought about by the moderate use of imprisonment and the greater use of fines and community sentences, and a reduction in delays. Fairness was seen in terms of equal opportunities and a better understanding of issues of race and gender; consistency in sentencing; and greater transparency in decision-making, including the giving of reasons. More recently, ideas of efficiency and fairness have been obscured by a political emphasis on "changing the balance" away from the offender, and (supposedly) in favour of the victim, for example, by measures designed to achieve a greater number of convictions; on more severe sentencing, justified by the slogan "prison works"; and on the introduction of more punitive elements into the administration of sentences served either in prison or in the community.

Issues of efficiency and fairness will certainly be no less important than they have been in the past. There will be a continuing need to make the best use of new technology, improve detection rates, minimise delays, raise standards, measure performance and control costs. There will always be pressure to do more with less. As regards fairness, issues such as miscarriages of justice, sensitivity to race and gender, consistent and principled sentencing, explanations for decisions, and arrangements for hearing grievances and putting them right, must continue to hold the attention of Parliament, government, the services and the courts. Both sets of issues will have to be reconciled, often with difficulty, in new policy initiatives, new legislation enacted by Parliament, the operational practice of the services, the administrative and judicial practice of the courts, and the professional practice of the legal and sometimes the medical and other professions. Distinctions between "policy" and "operations" will be difficult to sustain in any practical sense. The conflict will often reflect the contrast between the "inclusive" and "exclusive" values of society and justice, and the "high trust" and "low trust" views of management and organisations described in the first chapter.

The Police

For the police, the issues come together in the increasing practice of "profiling" and targeting known offenders in an attempt to increase clear up rates and reduce crime (Audit Commission 1993; Home Office 1996a). The Metropolitan Police operation "Bumblebee" is one example, and there are similar examples in other police areas. Operations are sometimes co-ordinated with local authorities in efforts both to reduce crime and to prevent its re-occurrence through comprehensive measures to improve the local environment, as in the King's Cross area of London. The police have claimed considerable success for these methods, attributing to them at least part of the fall in recorded crime which has taken place in the last three years. There seems to be no firm foundation for the sceptical view that the effect is only to displace crime to other areas, and if the improvement is genuine, it is to be profoundly welcomed.

There are, however, grounds for concern that methods of this kind could lead to justified criticisms of victimisation or harassment, or to the temptation for police officers to bend the rules in order to obtain the conviction of a person whom the "know" to be guilty. The result, which senior police officers are the first to recognise, would be a serious loss of public confidence and goodwill, especially if the operations appeared to be directed towards a particular ethnic group (Police Foundation/Policy Studies Institute 1996). Similar issues arise in relation to the powers provided by the Police and Public Order Act 1994 and by the Prevention of Terrorism (Additional Powers) Act 1996; to those proposed in the Asylum and Immigration Bill now before Parliament; and to the development of new technology. Methods, powers and equipment of the kinds that are now being developed need to be used within a framework of clear local and national accountability and absolute professional integrity (see Chapter X below). Vigilance will be needed to see whether the existing framework needs to be reinforced by more formal, possibly statutory, safeguards.

Another area of possible concern is the recent change in the law relating to the right of silence and the wording of the new police caution, and the intended change relating to the disclosure of evidence (in the Criminal Procedure and Investigations Bill now before Parliament). From one point of view, more serious criminals will be convicted and innocent or vulnerable suspects or defendants will have nothing to fear. On another view, argued by many lawyers, the innocent and vulnerable are more likely to be intimidated, with the risk of more miscarriages of justice; while experienced criminals will develop a new line of argument based on attacking the integrity of the police with expensive and time consuming "trials within trials", or Newton hearings to establish the validity or admissibility of their claims. Similar questions will arise over any further proposals relating to the admissibility of evidence such as hearsay or previous convictions (ACPO 1995).

A third instance concerns the readiness of the police to exercise their new powers under the public order provisions of the Criminal Justice and Public Order Act 1994 (those relating to demonstrators, squatters, travellers and "raves"); and the costs of doing so, both financially and in terms of public support (Penal Affairs Consortium 1995f). There seems to be considerable variation in practice between different areas (Mills H 1995).

A more general, and in some ways more fundamental, set of questions relates to the effect of national objectives, and of targets and performance indicators, together with the associated national political pressures, on the culture and style of local policing. These may well affect, and be intended to affect, the important balance between preventive and problem solving policing and the law enforcement (Fielding 1996) and crime control models discussed in Chapters I and IV. They may also involve conflicts of judgement, and possibility of loyalties, among members of police authorities. The indications are, however, that the new arrangements set in place by the Police and Magistrates' Courts Act 1994 have the potential to generate patterns of local policing which are imaginative, accountable and responsive. Those patterns would be achieved through the setting of local budgets and policing plans, and through local strategies to develop partnerships which the public, especially of police authorities, local authorities, other services, and the wider public can all be actively involved (Police Foundation/Policy Studies Institute 1996; Newburn and Jones 1996; Home Office 1996a).

Crown Prosecution Service

The Crown Prosecution Service had a difficult start from its origins in the Prosecution of Offenders Act 1985; and it has had a difficult history, especially as regards its relationships with the police and to some extent with the courts. Outside the system, it is relatively little known. But it has the potential to become a significant new force, both in managing or co-ordinating the criminal justice process; and in contributing to the development of national policy, for example, by exploring alternative means of resolving criminal cases outside the normal system or representing the interests of victims. It also has the capacity to affect sentencing, most obviously through the Attorney General's references to the Court of Appeal, but also through the choice of charge, the acceptance of pleas, and the increasingly prevalent process of plea and charge bargaining. Many of the concerns affecting the police, including the effect of performance indicators will apply equally to the Crown Prosecution Service (Sanders 1994b). Its actual, and still more its potential, influence on the system's efficiency, integrity and humanity is very considerable. As a government department which is non-political but whose functions are politically sensitive and which reports to a government Minister, it has an unusual constitutional position.

The Service seems for the present to be preoccupied with matters of its own internal procedures and operations, and with its relationships with the police, the courts and the practising legal profession (Home Office 1996a). Over the next few years, it will be increasingly important for the working and influence of the Crown Prosecution Service to be accessible and open to scrutiny; and for its longer term role in the development of the criminal justice system, and the nature and safeguards of its independence, to be carefully planned and clearly defined. The Service's relationship with, and responsibility, for victims (see Chapter VI) raises important questions of practice and principle. Perhaps the most fundamental issue is whether the Service is to be seen as an adjudicator or as a support to the police in achieving the maximum number of convictions by the most efficient means; or whether as the Royal Commission on Criminal Procedure and this Government originally intended, it should operate as an independent check on the police in cases where there is evidence of malpractice, selective enforcement, insensitivity or inconsistency. If the former, the Service would be reinforcing an "exclusive" view, if the latter, it could establish a creative tension between the "inclusive" and "exclusive" approaches.

Probation

Obvious issues for the probation service arise from the proposals in the green paper *Strengthening Punishment in the Community* (Home Office 1995e); and from the Government's intention to change the qualifications required for entry to the service, and in particular, to abolish the requirement to hold a post-graduate diploma in social work. Other concerns are the service's relationships, or partnerships, with other statutory and voluntary agencies including voluntary organisations, in providing services for offenders under supervision; the uncertain future of the service's work in prisons and with offenders after release; and a range of professional, managerial and technical matters affecting the service's work both with offenders and families, and its procedures and organisation.

Underlying all these issues is a more fundamental question about the nature and purpose of work with offenders in the community, the means by which it should be organised and delivered, and the services possible wider role in promoting social stability.

The view taken until, roughly, the 1970s was that the nature of the service's work was individual social casework, and its purpose was rehabilitation and social reintegration. This is still the view of many probation officers. But government and probation managers have increasingly imposed upon it a "crime control" or "public protection" view of the service's functions and a collective managerial approach. Early influences included the introduction of community service, increasing scepticism about the effectiveness of social work treatment and greater specialisation. More recent influences have been the development of probation service standards and performance indicators, and the political emphasis placed on the punitive aspects of supervision in the community. Some probation officers see themselves as "case mangers" overseeing and co-ordinating the provision of particular services by others: others still see themselves as individual caseworkers. There are considerable variations in the practice which results from the two approaches (Burnett 1996). Supervision has to be justified by a reduction in re-offending, and has to be shown to "work" in those terms (May 1994).

The Service has in most respects responded successfully to the challenges to its professionalism and its effectiveness. It is better known, more widely respected, and locally more influential than at any time in its history. It has more offenders under its supervision (about three times the number who are in prison). But the Government, the courts and some sections of the media do not see supervision as a real "punishment" and there is the sense of an underlying, and largely undefined, lack of confidence which the Government seems to share and sometimes to promote. The result is a green paper on *Strengthening Punishment in the Community* which not only repeats the insistence on the punitive aspects of supervision but also seems to define punishment exclusively in terms of the deliberate imposition of hardship or even humiliation. There is little regard for rehabilitation, personal influence, encouragement or opportunity, and all the emphasis is on compliance with requirements and the threat of imprisonment. At the same time the Government's proposal on qualifying training (Home Office 1994) seem to imply that the main tasks required of a probation officer are to enforce compliance and report failure.

Taken together the two sets of proposals imply a bleak and "exclusive" (see Chapter II) view of society and human nature. The challenge to the service, and the system and the community as a whole, is to develop a broadly based pattern of provision for the prevention of crime and the treatment of offenders; to include elements which will be recognised as punishment but relating them to the offender's life as a whole, and to the family, household and community in which the offender has to make his or her life. A similar challenge faces the health service in developing patterns of primary and community care (World Health Organisation 1984). Once the challenge is recognised and accepted, more specific objectives and tasks will begin to fall into place. The service must continue to develop programmes to reduce re-offending and to develop cognitive skills and identify "what works" (McGuire 1995), building for example, on the work which has been done in Hereford and Worcester (Hereford and Worcester Probation Service 1996), with regard to the hazards and limitations of that approach (Hood 1995). The priorities should not include legislation to change the powers of the courts or the structure of community sentences. But they should certainly include professional training which is based in higher education and independently validated; effective partnerships, with flexible and stable funding, between probation services and other agencies in the statutory and independent sectors; and a continuous process of research, exploration and service development. The newly formed Probation Studies Centre, associated with the Oxford Centre for Criminological Research, will have an important contribution to make (Travis 1996).

Prisons

Four years ago, the Prison Service enjoyed a brief period of optimism and confidence of a kind which few of its members could have known in their working lifetime. The prison population had fallen from over 50,000 to a little over 40,000. The Criminal Justice Act 1991 offered the prospect of a relatively stable population, held at an manageable level. "Fresh Start" had produced a plan for a more equitable system for pay and attendance for duty, without the destructive reliance on overtime which had so damaged the service in the past. The Woolf Report (Home Office 1991a), accepted by the Government in most important respects (Home Office 1991c), showed how the demands of security and control could be brought together with those of justice to provide constructive regimes for prisoners, and rewarding careers for staff. The transition of agency status provided a basis for its service to assert its own identity and individuality, and to become free from the frustrations of detailed political and central government control (Pilling 1992).

The next two years saw a satisfying fall in the number of prisoners held in overcrowded conditions, and an increase in those with access to night sanitation (with a virtual end to practice of slopping out), and in the opportunities for constructive activity.

43

Actual and Projected Prison Population 1980-2002

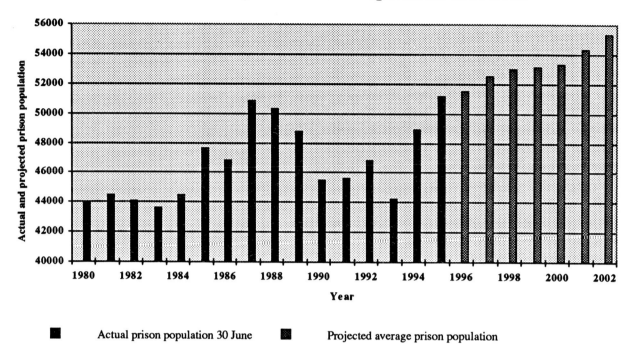

Actual prison population 30 June   Projected average prison population

Source: HM Prison Service Corporate Plan 1995-1998
Prison Statistics 1980-1994

It is sad that the service should again be facing a crisis of overcrowding, of failures in security, and of precarious control; that the improvements in regimes should be at risk; and that agency status should in the event have brought an unprecedented degree of political involvement in the management of the service, the damaging effects of which have been outlined in the Learmont Report (Home Office 1995c). It is ironic that these policies, and the effects on the Prison Service, should have been associated with the slogan "prison works," and with a spurious distinction between "policy" (for Ministers) and "operations" (for the Service) in which it is made to appear legitimate for policy to be formulated without regard to its operational consequences. It is also ironic that the Service's own skills, commitment, professionalism and sense of public service and public duty, however under-valued they may have become, should so often have prevented the overwhelming disasters which alone seem capable of generating the political will for a sustained programme of progress and reform.

A tempting solution is to call for a return to the policies and the situation as they were in 1992. But that is unrealistic. Whether or not those policies and that situation could have been sustained at that time, events have moved on too far for them to be restored in 1996. A lasting solution may now require more fundamental and longer term changes in the accountability, structure and culture of the system. The immediate task is however to restore stability and confidence, and not to embark on an unsettling fundamental reorganisation. Short term action may therefore have to be confined to tactical measures of the kind which have been characteristic of so much of prison administration since the Mountbatten Report nearly 30 years ago. But the guiding principles, however traditional they may seem, should include the following:

- Punishment is a matter for the courts, not for the Prison Service. The content of prison regimes should not be made deliberately unpleasant and degrading as a means a reinforcing the sentence's punitive effect;

- Prisoners are still citizens and human beings, to be regarded as having equal worth as people with other members of the prison community, although their position is necessarily different in terms of authority and status;

- They should be able to function as responsible citizens in the wider community to the extent that they are not prevented by the fact of their imprisonment (Lord Wilberforce's judgement in Raymond v Honey 1983 1AC1);

- Like the probation service, the Prison Service should explore "what works" in terms of preventing re-offending; the Prison Service should also develop performance indicators for pre-release preparations and other procedures and activities designed for this purpose;

- Within the law, and the policy as approved by Parliament, the treatment of individual prisoners should be a matter of professional or managerial and not of political judgement; and

- The prison population should be stabilized, and held at a level which matches the existing or planned capacity of the system.

Looking further ahead, the aims should be to establish a closer understanding of the respective roles and responsibilities of Ministers, the central Home Office and the Service itself, recognising that a distinction between "policy" and "operational" cannot be sustained in practice; to consider in particular the creation of an intermediate body such as an independent advisory board, as recommended by Admiral Sir Raymond Lygo in 1993 (Home Office 1993b), or a development in the role of Her Majesty's Chief Inspector of Prisons; and to permit and encourage a greater degree of diversity within the system so that different standards and procedures can be applied, for example, to women and young offenders (Williams 1996). Structures such as local boards should be developed to achieve a greater degree of accountability to local communities.

The Service should be relieved of all responsibility for the detention of young people under 18 (Howard League 1995f). Pending the abolition of the mandatory life sentence for murder, the arrangements for the release of prisoners serving mandatory life sentences should be brought into line with those serving discretionary life sentences (Windlesham 1996). To the extent that the commercial and independent sectors are to be involved at all in the work of prisons, their flexibility and resources should be used to develop new and imaginative prison structures and activities, and not to replace or compete with the national Prison Service in performing its traditional functions. Above all, the involvement of private sector operators must not be allowed to generate a "politics" of imprisonment in which their commercial interests come to have either an open or a subtle and insidious influence on policy, legislation and practice.

The new arrangements, roles and relationships, and the new structure of central and local accountability, should be placed on a statutory footing with a new and comprehensive Prison Act.

CHAPTER IX

The Courts and Sentencing

There is always the possibility of tension, between the Government on the one hand and the courts and the practising legal profession on the other, in any constitutional arrangement which involves the separation of powers. The courts will naturally, and properly, wish to preserve their independence and freedom from external constraint; the Government will be concerned about questions of efficiency and cost - both of the courts themselves, and of giving effect to their decisions. Parliament provides a (theoretically) independent authority which both respect, but it is largely controlled by the government of the day.

Tensions when they arise can concern the administration or funding of the courts and the legal process, including the operation of legal aid; cases in which Government decisions are challenged in the courts, for example, by way of judicial review; and the exercise of, or the constraints upon, the courts' discretion in matters such as sentencing. Such tensions are by no means new, but they have become more frequent and more intense during the last 10 or 15 years. The courts cannot expect to be exempt from the financial and economic constraints on the use and commitment of resources which are a necessary discipline in any modern society; but the Government should not expect the courts to act as its instruments or agents in seeking to achieve its political objectives, or to refrain from acting on complaints of injustice or unreasonable behaviour when they are brought before them. There will be no winners or public benefit in a situation where tension or a dispute remains unresolved, and still less in a situation where conflict is unnecessarily provoked.

In the context of criminal justice, the most difficult issues for the courts are likely for those involved in sentencing and in dealing with the increasingly complicated situations in which sentencing decisions have to be made. These situations include interpreting and applying the provisions of successive Criminal Justice Acts; and developing, interpreting and applying the Court of Appeal's guideline judgments and the Magistrates' Association's sentencing guidelines. All this has to be done in a context of unpredictable but often punitive and vocal public opinion and political pressure, in which it is hard (and may take some courage) to distinguish genuine public concern from populist exploitation. Areas of particular difficulty include the public and political demand, reflected in the Criminal Justice and Public Order Act 1994, for an increasingly punitive attitude towards children and young people; the use to be made of an offender's previous record and the extent to which previous offences should be treated as an aggravating factor; the weight to be given to the psychological impact on the victim and any statement made by the victim or on the victim's behalf; the status and purpose of community sentences; and the extent, if any, to which the availability of accommodation in prisons should influence sentencing practice.

All these issues, apart from the position of the victim, were prominent in discussions on sentencing during the 1980s. The hope was that they would be resolved in the Criminal Justice Act 1991 and the measures associated with it, but the Government's and the courts' retreat from the principles of that Act has produced a situation in which the issues must soon be reopened and re-examined. Such a re-examination will be essential if sentencing is to have any coherence or consistency; if the prison population is to be contained within the accommodation available or planned; and if the criminal justice system as a whole is to achieve any long time stability.

The difficulty of resolving these issues will be compounded if legislation is enacted to require the courts to pass mandatory minimum sentences of imprisonment for second convictions for certain sexual and violent offences; and mandatory minimum sentences of three or seven years for third convictions for offences of domestic burglary or drug trafficking, as proposed in the White Paper *Protecting the Public* (Home Office 1996a). Serious injustice would result for some individuals, and the trial process would be thrown into confusion if defendants no longer had an incentive to plead guilty, in the expectation of receiving a lighter sentence (there is a plaintive request for suggestions on how this might be retained); if more bargains were struck out of court; and if juries refused to convict in cases where they felt some sympathy for the defendant. Mandatory life sentences could put the general public, and the police and prison services at risk from offenders who thought they no longer had anything to lose. The proposals are in direct conflict with the long standing principle (not always, it has to be said, consistently applied in practice) that sentencing should not automatically increase in severity for a second and subsequent offences; and although the intended effect is limited to the range of offences stated, the courts might well come to impose similar sentences for other offences which they consider to be similarly serious. It is difficult to see how the courts could make sense of a discretion for "genuinely exceptional circumstances" in any way which would be consistent with the intention of the proposals, and there would be a period of uncertainty and confusion while the provision was being tested in particular cases.

The hope must be that the next Parliament will see, not the extension of mandatory sentences of new types of case, but the abolition of the existing mandatory sentence for murder and the injustice which is associated with it (House of Lords 1989; Windlesham 1993; Prison Reform Trust 1993; Howard League 1995d; JUSTICE forthcoming).

There may be a case for improving the arrangements for assessing the risk which potentially dangerous offenders are likely to present to the public at the point when they would otherwise be released, and for continuing their detention, subject to suitable safeguards, for the public's protection. It is arguable that this effect can be achieved under the existing provisions of sections 2 and 44 of the Criminal Justice Act 1991, without the need either to require the courts to impose a life sentence in cases where they would not, in the ordinary exercise of their discretion, think it necessary to do so, for example because it would be out of proportion to the seriousness of the actual offence. An alternative would be a "reviewable" sentence, as proposed by the Labour Party (Straw 1996), but again there would need to be safeguards to ensure that the offender was not being disproportionately punished on the basis of an unreliable assessment of the risk presented to the public. The issue should be first and foremost about the reliability and validity of the techniques of risk assessment, and only then about the statutory framework which should be applied. Extended and indeterminate sentences (preventive detention, borstal and corrective training) have been abandoned in the past because they did little to protect the public and were often unjust to the individuals concerned. The techniques of risk assessment may have improved over the years, but it has not been argued that they have improved to the point where they can justify a new structure of sentencing and there is still some scepticism about their reliability (Hood 1995).

The Government's proposals for "honesty in sentencing" - that the term to be served in prison should correspond more closely to the sentence as stated in court - has some attraction both to the courts and in terms of public presentation. It makes sense for sentences to "mean what they say". But it is important to distinguish the presentational arguments from the substantive effect. The present structure of a prison sentence of twelve months or more provides, quite deliberately, for a period to be spent in custody, and for a further period to be spent on licence in the community, with a liability to be fined or recalled if the offender fails to comply with the terms of the licence. Misunderstanding, and misinterpretation, could be avoided if the nature of the sentence were explained in more detail at the time when it is pronounced in court (Straw 1996). The existing provisions have been regarded as providing an important protection for the public as well as support for the prisoner in helping to avoid re-offending. Their substance should not be discarded for the sake of a purely presentational advantage.

The White Paper indicates that the Government does not expect this part of its proposals to result in a general increase in the time which offenders spend in prison, and that the result would be achieved either by a Practice Direction from the Lord Chief Justice or by a specific statutory provision. Recent history does not suggest that either method is likely to be effective.

The Government estimates that the progressive implementation of its proposals will result in an eventual increase in the prison population of about 10,800 by the year 2011-12. The White Paper does not say whether this increase includes or is in addition to the rise in the population - to 59,900 by the year 2004 - which is already projected on the basis of existing patterns of crime, detection and sentencing (Home Office 1996b), but it is presumably in addition. The White Paper also states that the estimate is based on three key assumptions. These are that "honesty in sentencing" will not lead to a general increase in the time which prisoners spend in custody; that mandatory sentences will have a deterrent effect such that the demand for prison places will fall by 20 per cent; and that there will be no significant effect on sentences for offences not directly covered by the proposals themselves. No evidence or argument is given to support these assumptions and all recent experience suggests that they are unreliable if not totally unrealistic. Not only that, but any legislation for greater severity in sentencing is likely - as in the United States and in this country during the past three years - to result in a general and accelerating increase in the severity of sentences and in the prison population, which future governments and future generations of the judiciary will find difficult to halt, let alone reverse.

As regards community sentences the green paper *Strengthening Punishment in the Community* proposed the amalgamation of the existing probation, community service and combination orders into a single sentence, with the court having the responsibility to determine, and presumably where necessary to vary, the particular requirements to be imposed on an offender in an individual case (Home Office 1995c). It is difficult to see how this responsibility can be regarded as a matter of judicial rather than a professional judgement. The respective roles of the courts and of the reporting probation officer or social worker could become seriously confused if the proposal is pursued. This is only one of a number of difficulties associated with the green paper if its proposals are enacted in legislation (Ashworth et al 1995; Howard League 1995e). It is reassuring that the more recent white paper does not propose early legislation on this subject, and concentrates on local demonstration projects to explore the scope for changes in approach by the courts and by the probation service.

Rather than attempt further piecemeal changes in criminal laws and criminal justice legislation, Parliament should concentrate on the progressive enactment of a complete and up to date criminal code as the Law Commission and the Association of Chief Police Officers have recommended (Law Commission 1989; 1993; ACPO 1995). Both have drawn attention to the frustration which the law enforcement services, the legal profession and the courts experience as a result of the inconsistency and obscurity of important parts of the existing criminal law.

Drawing on this experience and the Law Commission's proposals, Parliament should undertake a rigorous and principled review of the scope and structure of the criminal law, avoiding so far as possible the creation or retention of criminal offences which are intended for purely regulatory purposes (JUSTICE 1980), or to control social problems or problems of relationships. The former could often be resolved rather better by other means such as administrative penalties and the latter by alternative procedures such as mediation or conciliation. Parliament should also avoid the creation of absolute offences, where for example the offence charged is defined as a failure to comply with police instructions, as a means of making convictions easier to obtain.

CHAPTER X

Accountability, Co-operation, Structure and Relationships

Previous chapters have pointed to four main themes which have to be developed if confidence and a sense of progress and direction are to be restored. They are accountability, co-operation, structure, and relationships.

Accountability

A great deal has been said and written during the past ten years about accountability in the public services. Important features for the purpose of this paper are the increasing centralisation of power in the political administration of the day, combined with and reinforced by the increasing devolution of responsibility to local managers; the emphasis on financial accountability to central government and the achievement of centrally determined performance targets; and a contractual or consumerist view of accountability to the wider public which concentrates on public information and opportunities to complain or demand compensation. Parliamentary control seems to many people increasingly ineffective and irrelevant; and (except for the police) little attention is paid to any sense of accountability to local populations or communities. Sophisticated, and some would say spurious, distinctions are made between "policy" and "operations" and between "accountability" and "responsibility".

The new construction of accountability has brought important benefits in terms of efficiency and economy; in clarity of objectives (but not always in clarity of purpose); and in the volume of information which is publicly available (although it may not always be found relevant or easy to interpret). It is based on a culture of accountancy and audit. The Audit Commission has produced important reports on the police and the probation services (Audit Commission 1989; 1991; and 1994) which have made a significant contribution to those services' managerial and professional development. But this attitude to accountability also reinforces the wider political culture of short-term objectives, of concentrating on what is immediate and practical rather than principled, strategic or long term; of risk assessment and risk avoidance; and of blame and punishment for failure. The Citizen's Charter and the charters related to it have had some success in raising service providers' awareness of the interests and feelings of those who use, or come into contact with, the services - for example victims of crime or those who have to go to court. It has not given them much sense of control or influence, of ownership or empowerment or even of choice, and the language itself causes difficulty as

51

soon as it reaches a conceptual level. The sense of powerlessness is probably as great in respect of the criminal justice system as it is for any other public service.

Effective accountability requires all or most of the following:

- appointments made openly and on merit;
- accessible and well understood procedures for public consultation;
- clearly stated objectives, standards and expectations;
- monitoring of performance to establish how far those objectives are being met;
- independent inspection and audit;
- reasons for decisions explained to those affected by them;
- opportunities and a recognised structure for representations and complaints;
- effective means for correcting mistakes, abuses or errors of judgement and for preventing them form bcing repeated, but not an obsession with blaming and punishing individuals;
- informative, well-presented published reports;
- recognition of, and sensitivity to, issues of race, gender and culture; and
- a statutory of framework within which these requirement can ultimately be enforced through the courts.

A necessary condition for these requirements is a sense that accountability - or responsibility - should lie, not just to central government and Parliament, but also to local communities, to the institutions and organisations within them, and to individuals. Accountability should take multiple forms and operate throughout multiple channels.

Services or institutions which exercise coercive powers must be not only accountable but also legitimate. They must function with the consent and support of society as a whole. The authority of those who exercise them has to be respected in its own right and not simply imposed on those made subject to them. Police cannot function without the consent of the public, and prisons cannot, in the last resort function without the consent of the inmates. This point was acknowledged, but not developed, in the White Paper *Punishment and Supervision in the Community* (Home Office 1990a). It was discussed more fully in the Woolf Report on prisons (Home Office 1991), where it became a major theme; and it has been explored academically by Anthony Bottoms and Richard Sparks (Bottoms 1994; Sparks and Bottoms 1995).

All the criminal justice services, and the courts, should consider how far they can be considered accountable, and legitimate, by the standards indicated in this chapter. The police, the magistrates' courts, and the probation services are locally based and have a structure which permits a degree of local accountability so far as it is not constrained by central government requirements. There may, however, be room to develop local structures and procedures which would make their accountability more effective and these shall be explored. There should, in particular, be a representative police authority for London, and a clearly defined structure of accountability for the Security Service if it is to become involved in measures against organised crime.

The Crown Prosecution Service, the higher courts and the Prison Service are all centrally managed and directed, with different degrees of political control, and forms of regional or local organisation. To the extent that they have a regional organisation, it is designed only to serve the purposes of internal management. There is no relationship between their boundaries and those of other services, or with the natural structure of the communities they serve. All three should seek to develop a greater sense of identity and accountability with those communities, establishing suitable procedures and structures for this purpose, and common boundaries so far as it is practicable to do so (Police Foundation/Policy Studies Institute 1996).

Co-operation

Co-operation, inter-agency working and partnerships have been important themes in crime prevention and criminal justice since the early 1980s. Reasons include the drive for efficiency and economy, mentioned in Chapter XI, and the recognition of the complexity of the issues involved in preventing crime, supporting victims and managing the system described in Chapters VI-IX. Even so, there is more still to be done, and the problems and the tasks change as the situation changes in the country, and as circumstances change in the different services. Financial pressures, rigorous application of performance indicators, concentration on "core" or statutory functions, turnover of staff and changes in organisation, can all conspire to create an inward-looking, service-centred outlook, and to discourage work with other agencies which may appear to be of marginal benefit to the service or the individual concerned. Differences in outlook and culture, or ordinary ignorance of other services' work, can be a further discouragement.

These difficulties are now generally understood and widely recognised, but it takes continuous effort to overcome them, even in those services which are used to working together within the criminal justice system (examples have been given in the previous chapter). Even greater efforts are needed to sustain joint working between criminal justice services and those which do not see themselves as part of the system - health, social services, education, housing, social security, and voluntary organisations of various kinds. This wider form of co-operation is of critical importance in the increasingly complex situation in which crime comes to be committed and criminal justice has to be administered.

Co-operation has to take place at least three levels:

- Policies have to be co-ordinated between departments within central government;

- Priorities and working arrangements have to be co-ordinated at a planning level between different services; and

- Practice has to be co-ordinated at a local level between different practitioners.

Reliable information and systematic analysis are essential ingredients at each level. Academic institutions and the business community have important contributions to make. Examples of subjects where the need has been recognised and progress has been made include the abuse of drugs, with the 1995 White Paper (Home Office et al 1995); and mental health (Home Office/Department of Health 1992; Home Office 1995d). But the links between ill health and criminality, or more positively, between public health and public safety, are still not adequately recognised or taken fully into account by health service commissioners or providers, and there is scope for more productive co-operation (Home Office 1996c; James forthcoming).

There is similar scope, and perhaps now increasing recognition (Home Office 1996a), in relation to social services, education and housing. In these areas the effect of financial constraints, organisational change and current and prospective policies and legislation are causing increasing frustration to those who see them as increasing the country's neglect of issues which are critical to its social stability and long term future.

Structure

It is all too easy to propose new structures and new procedures as if they would, by themselves, provide the solution to the problems under discussion. Not only that, but preoccupation with structures and procedures can too easily distract professional and managerial attention from the substantive problems for which solutions are being sought. Even so, the questions of accountability and co-ordination discussed earlier in this chapter, and the questions of analysis and judgement discussed earlier in this paper, suggest the need for more systematic and more firmly established arrangements than those which exist at present. The need was recognised in Lord Woolf's report on the prison disturbances in April 1990, and in the Government's acceptance of the recommendations for a national Criminal Justice Consultative Council and area criminal justice liaison committees which have now been established (Home Office 1991c). Other proposals have been for the establishment of a sentencing council (Ashworth 1983; Penal Affairs Consortium 1995b) and for the creation of a Ministry of Justice.

The Howard League for Penal Reform has put forward a more comprehensive set of proposals in its report on *The Dynamics of Justice* (Howard League 1993b). Many of the proposals in that report also flow naturally from the analysis in this Green Paper:

- The Criminal Justice Consultative Council would be formally recognised as a national forum for consultation and planning. It would be enabled to form committees to examine and report on particular issues. Its membership, including membership of the committees, would be widened to include academics, representatives of the religious communities and the voluntary sector, and others with relevant experience. With its advice, the Government would produce an annual, costed, strategic plan. The Council would be placed on a statutory basis.

- Area criminal justice committees would be developed in the same way at a more local level, and would be made more representative of local communities.

- Associated with the Council, but independent of government, a Criminal Justice Institute would provide a service of interpretation and analysis and a focus for professional and management studies. It would commission and publish research. It would organise seminars and training courses, including joint training for rising and senior practitioners from all criminal justice services and professions. It would work closely with universities and with the Judicial Studies Board. The Board itself would be developed to become a judicial college.

- A new legislative framework would be developed for the police, probation and prison services.

- The Law Commission would be systematically involved in the drafting of criminal justice legislation, with suitable public consultation.

These proposals should be adopted and put into effect.

Relationships

It is becoming increasingly recognised that successful outcomes depend to a large extent on the quality of the relationships among those engaged in the process which creates them. Many of the social and economic changes which have taken place in developed countries in the last 30 years have sought to increase efficiency by reducing human contact. Staff have been removed, procedures have been mechanised and the traditions of long service and personal loyalty have been destroyed or devalued. Organisations have become less personal. Families and communities have become fragmented (Schluter and Lee 1993). The underlying values have become increasingly those of an exclusive rather than an inclusive society, as described in Chapter II.

This fragmentation is almost certainly associated with the increase in crime and the problems of confidence discussed in Chapter I. Its effect is difficult to quantify, but the prevention of crime and criminality, and the operation of a system which is seen and experienced as fair and just, depend upon successful human relationships and are in a sense, an expression of them (Burnside and Baker 1994).

Changes in legislation, funding or management, and improvements in accountability, co-operation and structure, however important they may be, will therefore achieve very little unless they are founded on sound relationships, both between individuals and between organisations.

Practical applications of relational thinking are to be found in most areas of social and economic activity. Those which can most profitably be developed in the context of crime and criminal justice include:

- the relationships between staff and offenders in prison or under supervision, with particular reference to work on confronting offending behaviour but also to establishing mutual respect in day-to-day contact;

- the scope for establishing informal but influential relationships between offenders and mentors in their own communities, building on the experience of organisations such as the Divert Trust;

- relationships between offenders and victims, especially in situations which cannot be satisfactorily resolved by criminal procedures on their own (for example, some of those involving children), and where mediation or conciliation may produce more satisfactory results; and

- relationships between organisations which have to work together in partnership, where differences of organisation, tradition and professional culture have to be resolved on a basis of common information, equal status, and shared power and influence.

Relationships in the criminal justice system, and ultimately the quality of justice itself, depend on the commitment and skill of the first line staff through whom the services have to function. Much depends on the extent to which staff feel supported, valued, confident and secure. Those feelings will be influenced by the institutional framework in which they have to operate, and by the political, social and economic changes which take place within or are imposed upon that framework. The influences may be progressive in the sense of creating a will to adopt new ideas and approaches, and to do so in a spirit of optimism and confidence; or regressive in the sense of generating, or reinforcing, a climate of rigidity, fear, suspicion and exclusion (Freedland 1996; Snow 1996). The former are likely to be associated with a high trust approach to employment relationships, as described in Chapter II; the latter with an approach based on low trust and individual blame.

Influences over the last 15 years have been of both kinds. The task for the future is to maximise those influences which are progressive and minimise those which have negatives effects. Subjects meriting attention include:

- terms and conditions of service and the relationship between staff and their employing authorities;

- the extent to which they feel committed to the direction in which they perceive their work to be moving, and to which they feel able to influence it;

- their sense of personal and professional confidence, based on training and experience and the support of colleagues, including the confidence to take risks when necessary and justified, and not simply to recognise and avoid them; and

- confident and productive working relationships with all those with whom they come into working contact, based on understanding and mutual respect.

CHAPTER XI

Summary and Conclusions

This paper seeks to promote a thoughtful and principled debate about the nature and causes of crime; the means of preventing it and mitigating its effects; the purpose, operation and effectiveness of the criminal justice process; and the treatment of offenders.

It began by examining the state of public and professional confidence over the incidence of crime and the functioning of the criminal justice system, and the nature and quality of public and political debate. It argued that fear of crime and lack of confidence in the system have led to unrealistic expectations and over simplification of the issues, and to a concentration on law enforcement and punishment which may be effective as an expression of public feeling, but not as a means of reducing crime or dealing with its effects. This approach to crime is related to a more generally "exclusive" attitude to human behaviour and to society which is based on social division, personal protection, suspicion and fear. A contrasting "inclusive" view would value and respect diversity, human dignity, compassion and the will to change.

An analysis of crime and patterns of offending shows that most crimes are against property, and that violent and sexual crimes are very rare (if widely reported). Some experience of offending is common among young men: most grow out of it, but a few go on to become serious or persistent criminals. The same people can often be both offenders and victims and it is misleading to think of a separate criminal class. The origins of criminality are often to be found in early childhood. A serious programme to reduce it should focus on support for parents and children in difficulty, and opportunities for young people entering upon adult life. It should also recognise the too often neglected problems of mental disorder among children and adolescents. Programmes to prevent crime by physical means, including video cameras and closed circuit television, can be of value, but their effects will be limited and local unless action is also taken to change the motivation of offenders and those at risk of offending.

Welcome progress has been made in providing services and support for victims of crime. More needs to be done to give them the information and help, and the recognition and respect to which they are entitled. But proposals to involve them more directly in decisions affecting the lives and liberty of offenders should be approached with great caution.

Feasible changes in law enforcement and the criminal justice process, or in criminal law or the treatment of offenders, are by themselves unlikely to have more than a marginal effect on the general level of crime. Changes in police methods and higher detection rates can have an impact locally and should certainly be considered and evaluated. But changes in criminal procedure can be uncertain in their effect, and greater severity in sentencing and harsher conditions for those serving sentences are more likely to reinforce criminality than to reduce it. Rather than attempting further piecemeal changes in criminal law and criminal justice legislation, Parliament should seek to enact a coherent, comprehensive and comprehensible criminal code on the lines which the Law Commission has recommended.

All the criminal justice services are in a state of uncertainty and often confusion as they adjust themselves to the rapid changes which have been imposed upon them in the recent past, and as they try to anticipate the further changes which can be expected in the future. Immediate tasks are to sustain public and professional confidence, and to maintain and improve the services' operational effectiveness. But effectiveness is hard to define in more than narrow managerial terms, and all the services, and the courts, have to balance wider and often conflicting considerations and priorities.

For the police, the balance is between a "public service" and a "crime control" view of policing: between national priorities and local needs; between intensive law enforcement and targetting "known offenders", and loss of public support through complaints of oppression and harassment; between rigorous methods to identify and convict sophisticated criminals, and the protection of the weak and vulnerable; and between maintaining a public presence and concentration on measures likely to maximise arrests and convictions.

For the Crown Prosecution Service the balance is between securing a high rate of convictions, and the police and sometimes the victim's interest in letting the case reach the courts and allowing the courts to decide - a balance which can sometimes be seen as a conflict between operational efficiency and public confidence. Longer term issues affecting the Service include its relationship with the police during a police investigation, its responsibilities towards victims, and the possible development of its function in relation to sentencing.

For the courts, the issues relate to the influence of public and political opinion on matters of judicial judgement; the means of achieving consistency with frequent changes of legislation; the relationship between judicial and professional judgement in matters relating to community sentences; and the procedures by which the operational and consequences of judicial decisions can be reconciled with the means and resources available to put them into effect. Issues of a more general kind arise over the recognition to be given to victims or in the handling of cases where other conflicts, for example over the integrity or acceptability of police methods, have to be resolved in court. Further issues, and the possibility of serious injustice and confusion, will arise if legislation is enacted for minimum mandatory sentences.

For the probation service, the main conflict is between changing behaviour and enforcing compliance as the focus of the service's work with offenders. There are important implications for the organisation of probation services, for their relations and partnerships with other services and organisations, and for the professional qualifications and training required for probation officers. Other issues concern the service's relationship with the courts in relation to community sentences and the future of its work in prisons and with prisoners after release.

The most immediate issues for the Prison Service concern its own stability in a context of a rapidly rising prison population, increasing politicisation of prison regimes and an uncertain relationship between the Service and the central Home Office and the political administration of the day. All these should eventually be addressed in legislation, possibly involving a more radical reconstruction of the Prison Service than has so far been contemplated. But legislation should be approached carefully, with wide-ranging consultation and discussion, and the Service should be spared another organisational upheaval until operational stability has been restored. In the meantime, a number of principles should be established or re-established as a foundation both for the Service's day to day policy and operations, and for the legislation which would be enacted in due course.

Four important themes emerge from the analysis in this paper:

1. The Government, the services and the courts should recognise that the system needs to be accountable not only to central government but also locally to the communities which it serves.

2. The system still needs to be co-ordinated more effectively within itself, and with other services and agencies whose work is crucial to its success.

3. Structures and procedures need to be established to ensure that the system's accountability and co-ordination is effective, and that decisions are taken on the basis of accurate information and analysis. Co-ordination is needed at three levels: politically and strategically at central government level, professionally and managerially at service level, and operationally between individual teams and practitioners.

4. The efficiency of the system, and ultimately the quality of the justice, depend on the commitment and skill of first line staff and on the nature of their professional and working relationships.

REFERENCES

Advisory Council on the Penal System (1974) *Report on Young Adult Offenders,* London, HMSO

Ashworth (1983) *Sentencing and Penal Policy,* London, Weidenfeld and Nicholson

Ashworth A (1993) *Victim Impact Statements and Sentencing,* Criminal Law Review, 1993, p498

Ashworth A (1995a) *Sentencing and Criminal Justice,* London, Weidenfeld and Nicholson

Ashworth A (1995b) *Matters of Chance: Offenders, Victims and the Luck of the Draw,* Criminal Justice Matters No. 22

Ashworth A (1996) *Crime, Community and Creeping Consequentialism,* Criminal Law Review, 1996, p220

Ashworth A, von Hirsch A, Bottoms A & Wasik M (1995) *Bespoke Tailoring Won't Suit Community Sentences,* New Law Journal 30 June 1995

Association of Chief Officers of Police (1990) *Setting the Standards for Policing: Meeting Community Expectations.* Report of a Working Party including representatives of ACPO, the Superintendents Association, the Police Federation and the Home Office, London, ACPO

Association of Chief Officers of Police (1995) *In Search of Criminal Justice: A Position Paper for ACPO on the Criminal Justice System,* London, ACPO

Audit Commission (1990) *Effective Policing: Performance Review in Police Forces,* London, Audit Commission

Audit Commission (1991) *Going Straight: Developing Good Practice in the Probation Service,* London, Audit Commission

Audit Commission (1993) *Helping with Enquiries: Tackling Crime Effectively,* London, HMSO

Audit Commission (1996) *Streetwise: Effective Police Patrol,* London, HMSO

Barrett J and Greenaway R (1995) *Why Adventure? A Review of Research Literature Relating to Outdoor Adventure,* Young People and their Personal and Social Development, Coventry, Foundation for Outdoor Adventure

Baxter R & Nuttall C (1975) *Severe Sentences: No Deterrent to Crime,* New Society, 2 January 1975

Blackstone W (1765) *Commentaries on the Laws of England*

Bottoms A (1994) *Avoiding Injustice, Promoting Legitimacy and Relationships,* in Burnside and Baker (eds) *Relational Justice,* Winchester, Waterside Press

Braithwaite J (1989) *Crime, Shame and Reintegration,* Cambridge University Press

Braithwaite J (1993) *Shame and Modernity,* British Journal of Criminology, Vol 33, No 1

Braithwaite J & Pettit P (1990) *Not Just Deserts: A Republican Theory of Criminal Justice,* Oxford, Clarendon Press

Brake M & Hale C (1992) *Public Order and Private Lives: The Politics of Law and Order,* London, Routledge

Brody S (1975) *The Effectiveness of Sentencing,* Home Office Research Study No. 35, London, HMSO

Burnett R (1994a) *Recidivism and Imprisonment,* Home Office Research Bulletin Special Edition, Prisons and Prisoners

Burnett R (1994b) *The Odds of Going Straight: Offenders' Own Predictions,* University of Oxford Centre for Criminological Research

Burnett R (1996) *Fitting Supervision to Offenders: Assessment and Allocation Decisions in the Probation Service,* Home Office Research Study No. 153, London, HMSO

Burnside J & Baker N (eds) (1994) *Relational Justice - Repairing the Breach*, Winchester, Waterside Press

Cavadino M & Dignan J (1992) *The Penal System: An Introduction*, London, Sage

Cervi B (1996) *Cautionary Tale*, Community Care, 7-13 March

Chunn L (1996) *Suffer the Children*, The Observer, 10 March 1996

Clarke R & Hough M (1984) *Crime and Police Effectiveness*, Home Office Research Study No. 79, London, HMSO

Cohen S (1985) *Visions of Social Control*, Oxford, Polity

Cohen S (1996) Lecture given at All Souls' College Oxford, 5 March 1996

Cornish D & Clarke R (eds) (1986) *The Reasoning Criminal: Rational Choice Perspectives on Offending*, New York, Springer Verlag

Department of Health and Department for Education (1995) *A Handbook on Child and Adolescent Mental Health*, London, Department of Health

Devlin A (1995) *Criminal Classes: Offenders at School*, Winchester, Waterside Press

Downes D & Morgan R (1994) *Hostages to Fortune ? The Politics of Law and Order in Post-war Britain* in Maguire M, Morgan R & Reiner R (eds) *The Oxford Handbook of Criminology* Oxford University Press

Farrington D (1994) *Human Development and Criminal Careers*, in Maguire et al, *The Oxford Handbook of Criminology*, Oxford University Press

Faulkner D (1995a) *The Criminal Justice Act 1991: Policy, Legislation and Practice*, in Ward D & Lacey N (eds) *Probation: Working for Justice*, London, Whiting and Birch

Faulkner D (1995b) *Law Citizenship and Responsibility: Teaching Children Right from Wrong*, Criminal Justice Vol 13 No 1 pp9-11, February 1995

Fawcett J (1985) *Applications of the European Convention on Human Rights*, in Maguire M, Vagg J & Morgan R (eds) *Accountability and Prisons*, London, Tavistock

Field S (1990) *Trends in Crime and their Interpretation: A Study of Post-war Crime in England and Wales*, Home Office Research Study No. 119, London, HMSO

Fielding N (1995) *Community Policing*, Oxford, Clarendon Press

Fox A (1974) *Beyond Contract: Work, Power and Trust Relations*, London, Faber and Faber

Freedland M (1994) *Government by Contract and Public Law*, Public Law, Spring 1994

Freedland M (1996) *Citizenship and New Models of Public Administration and Public Service*, Paper presented to the European University Institute's Workshop on Social and Political Citizenship in a World of Migration, February 1996

Gelsthorpe L & Morris A (1994) *Juvenile Justice 1945-1992* in Maguire et al, *The Oxford Handbook of Criminology*, Oxford University Press

Graef R (1992) *Living Dangerously: Young Offenders in their Own Words*, London, Harper Collins

Graham J & Bowling B (1996) *Young People and Crime*, Home Office Research Study No. 145, London, HMSO

Hagell A & Newburn T (1994) *Persistent Young Offenders*, London, Policy Studies Institute

Heal K (1991) *Changing Perspective on Crime Prevention: The Role of Information and Structure*, in Evans D, Fyfe N & Herbert D (eds) *Crime Policing and Place: Essays in Environmental Criminology*, London, Routledge

Health Advisory Service (1995) *A Thematic Review of Child and Adolescent Mental Health Services, "Together We Stand"*, London, Health Advisory Service

Hereford and Worcester Probation Service (1996) *Effective Supervision of Offenders*, Hereford and Worcester Probation Service

Hill D (1994) *Why the Lords Must Not Let Criminals Win*, Daily Express, 26 April 1994

Holman B (1995) *Children and Crime*, Oxford, Lion

Home Office (1977) *A Review of Criminal Justice Policy, 1976*, London, Home Office

Home Office (1979) *Report of the Committee of Inquiry into the United Kingdom Prison Services (May Report)*, Cmnd 7673, London, HMSO

Home Office (1984) *Criminal Justice: A Working Paper,* London, Home Office

Home Office (1988) *Punishment, Custody and the Community,* Cmnd 424, London, HMSO

Home Office (1990) *Crime, Justice and Protecting the Public,* Cm 965, London, HMSO

Home Office (1991a) *Prison Disturbances in April 1990: Report of an Inquiry by the Rt Hon Lord Justice Woolf (Parts I and II) and His Honour Judge Stephen Tumim (Part II)* Cm 1456, London, HMSO

Home Office (1991b) *Safer Communities: The Local Delivery of Crime Prevention through the Partnership Approach: Report of the Standing Conference on Crime Prevention (The Morgan Report),* London, HMSO

Home Office (1991c) *Custody, Care and Justice: The Way Ahead for the Prison Service in England and Wales,* Cm 1647, London, Home Office

Home Office (1991d) *Management of the Prison Service: Report by Admiral Sir Raymond Lygo,* London, Home Office

Home Office/Department of Health (1992) *Joint Review of Services for Mentally Disordered Offenders and Others Requiring Similar Services (The Reed Report/Final Summary),* Cm 2088, London. HMSO

Home Office (1993a) *Police Reform,* Cm 2281, London, HMSO

Home Office (1993b) *Compensation for Victims of Violent Crime: Changes in the Criminal Injuries Compensation Scheme,* Cm 2434, London, HMSO

Home Office (1994) *Review of Probation Officer Recruitment and Qualifying Training,* London, HMSO

Home Office (1995a) *Digest of Information on the Criminal Justice System in England and Wales No. 3,* London

Home Office (1995b) *Criminal Careers of Those Born between 1953 and 1973,* Home Office Statistical Bulletin 14/95, London, HMSO

Home Office (1995c) *Strengthening Punishment in the Community: A Consultation Document,* Cm 2780, London, Home Office

Home Office (1995d) *Review of Prison Service Security in England and Wales and the Escapes from Parkhurst Prison on Tuesday 3 January 1995: The Learmont Report,* Cm 3020, London, HMSO

Home Office (1995e) *Mentally Disordered Offenders: Inter-Agency Working,* Home Office Circular No 12/95

Home Office/ Department of Health/Department for Education (1995) *Tackling Drugs Together: A Strategy for 1995-98,* London, HMSO

Home Office (1996a) *Protecting the Public. The Government's Strategy on Crime in England and Wales,* Cm 3190, London, HMSO

Home Office (1996b) *Projections of Long Term Trends in the Prison Population to 2004,* Statistical Bulletin No 4/96, London, Home Office

Home Office (1996c) *A Guidance Document Aimed at Promoting Effective Working Between the Health and Probation Services,* London, Home Office

Hood R (1989) *The Death Penalty,* Oxford University Press

Hood R (1995) *Introductory Report to the Proceedings of the 20th Century Criminological and Psychological Interventions in the Criminal Justice System,* Strasbourg, Council of Europe Press

Hough M & Mayhew P (1983) *The British Crime Survey,* Home Office Research Study No. 76, London, HMSO

Hough M & Mayhew P (1985) *Taking Account of Crime: Key Findings from the Second British Crime Survey,* Home Office Research Study No. 85, London, HMSO

Hough M (1995) *Anxiety About Crime: Findings of the 1994 British Crime Survey,* London, HMSO

Howard League (1993a) *Young and In Trouble,* London, Howard League

Howard League (1993b) *Dynamics of Justice,* London, Howard League

Howard League (1995a) *Secure Training Orders: Repeating Failures of the Past*, London, Howard League

Howard League (1995b) *Troubleshooter: Report of a Project to Rescue 15 Year Olds From Prison*, London, Howard League

Howard League (1995c) *Child Offenders*, London, Howard League

Howard League (1995d) *Howard League submission to the Home Affairs Committee Inquiry into Murder and Life Imprisonment and the "Year and a Day" Rule*, London, Howard League

Howard League (1995e) *The Howard League's response to the Green Paper Strengthening Punishment in the Community*, London, Howard League

Howard League (1995f) *Banged Up, Beaten Up, Cutting Up: Report of a Commission of Inquiry into Violence in Penal Institutions for Teenagers Under 18*, London, Howard League

House of Lords (1989) *Report of the Select Committee on Murder and Life Imprisonment*, HL paper 78-1, London, HMSO

Hudson B (1987) *Justice Through Punishment: A Critique of the "Justice" Model of Corrections*, London, MacMillan

Hudson B (1993) *Penal Policy and Criminal Justice*, London, MacMillan

Huskins J (forthcoming) *Quality Youth Work - Empowering Young People and Diversion from Risk*, London, Youth Clubs UK

Hutton W (1995) *The State We're In*, London, Jonathan Cape

James A (forthcoming) *Life on the Edge*, London, Mental Health Foundation

Jenkins S (1995) *Accountable to None: The Tory Nationalization of Britain*, London, Hamish Hamilton

JUSTICE (1980) *Breaking the Rules: The Problem of Crimes and Contraventions*, London, JUSTICE

JUSTICE (1996) *Children and Homicide: Appropriate Procedures for Juveniles in Murder and Manslaughter Cases*, London, JUSTICE

JUSTICE (forthcoming) *Sentenced for Life*, London, JUSTICE

King R & McDermott K (1995) *The State of Our Prisons*, Oxford, Clarendon Press

Kurtz Z, Thanes R and Wolind S (1994) *Services for the Mental Health of Children and Young People in England*, London, Maudsley Hospital and South Thames Regional Health Authority

Lacey N (1994a) *Government as Manager, Citizen as Consumer*, Modern Law Review, Vol 57, No 4

Lacey N (1994b) *Missing the Wood ... Pragmatism and Theory in the Royal Commission*, in McConville M and Bridges L (eds) *Criminal Justice in Crisis*, Aldershot, Edward Elgar

Lacey N & Zedner L (1995) *Discourses of Community in Criminal Justice: Locating the Appeal to "Community" in Contemporary Criminal Justice*, Journal of Law and Society, Vol 22 No. 3

Law Commission (1989) A Criminal Code for England and Wales, London, HMSO

Law Commission (1993) *Legislating the Criminal Code: Offences Against the Person and General Principles*, London, HMSO

Leach P (1994) *Children First: What Our Society Must Do - And is Not Doing - for Our Children Today*, London, Michael Joseph

Leff S (1996) *Working Together to Identify Children in Need*, Health Visitor 69/1

Levi M (1994) *Violent Crime* in Maguire et al, *The Oxford Handbook of Criminology*, Oxford University Press

Locke J (1690) *Second Treatise of Civil Government*

Loveday B (1994) *Government Strategies for Community Crime Prevention in England and Wales a Study in Failure*, International Journal of the Sociology of Law, 1994, Vol 22, pp181-202

Loveday B (1995) *Reforming the Police: From Local Service to State Police?* Political Quarterly, 66(2)

McGuire J (ed) (1995) *What Works: Research and Practice on the Reduction of Re-offending*, Chichester, John Wyley and Sons

Maguire M (1980) *The Impact of Burglary upon Victims*, British Journal of Criminology Vol 20 No. 3

Maguire M (1994) *Crime Statistics, Patterns and Trends,* in Maguire et al (eds) *The Oxford Handbook of Criminology,* Oxford University Press

Maguire M, Vagg J & Morgan R (eds) (1985) *Accountability and Prisons: Opening Up a Closed World,* London, Tavistock

Marshall T & Merry S (1990) *Crime and Accountability: Victim/Offender Mediation in Practice,* London, HMSO

Martinson R et al (1974) *What Works? Questions and Answers about Prison Reform,* Public Interest 34

Martinson R (1979) *New Findings, New Views: A Note of Caution on Sentencing Reform,* Hofstra Law Review 7

Mawby R (1979) *The Victimisation of Juveniles.* The Journal of Crime and Delinquency, 1979, pp98-114

May T (1994) *Probation and Community Sanctions* in Maguire et al, *The Oxford Handbook of Criminology,* Oxford University Press

Mayhew P & Hough M (1988) *The British Crime Survey: Origins and Impact* in Maguire M & Pointing J (eds) *Victims of Crime: A New Deal?* Milton Keynes, Open University Press

Mayhew P & Aye Maung N (1992) *Surveying Crime: Findings from the 1992 British Crime Survey,* Home Office Research and Statistics Department, Research Findings No. 2, London, HMSO

Mayhew P, Aye Maung N & Mirlees-Black C (1993) *The 1992 British Crime Survey,* Home Office Research Study No. 132, London, HMSO

Mayhew P, Mirlees-Black C and Aye Maung N (1994) *Trends in Crime: Findings from the 1994 British Crime Survey,* Research Findings No. 14, London, HMSO

Maxfield M (1984) *Fear of Crime in England and Wales,* Home Office Research Study No. 78, London, HMSO

Mental Health Foundation (1995) *Fundamental Facts,* London, Mental Health Foundation

Mills B (1995) *Working Towards a Better Deal for Victims,* London, Victim Support

Mills H (1995) *It Takes a Bad Act to Make the Law a Farce,* The Independent, 26 September 1995

Morgan R (1994) *Imprisonment* in Maguire et al, *The Oxford Handbook of Criminology,* Oxford University Press

Morgan J & Zedner L (1992) *Child Victims,* Oxford, Clarendon Press

Morris A & Giller H (1987) *Understanding Juvenile Justice,* London, Croome Helm

Moxon D (1985) *Managing Criminal Justice,* London, HMSO

NACRO (1995) *Crime and Social Policy,* London, NACRO

Nelken D (1995) *Community Involvement in Crime Control* in Maguire et al, *The Oxford Handbook of Criminology,* Oxford University Press

Nellis M (1995) *Probation Values for the 1990s,* The Howard Journal of Criminal Justice, Vol 34, No 1

Newburn T & Jones T (1996) *Police Accountability,* in Salisbury W, Mott J & Newburn T (eds) *Themes in Contemporary Policing,* London, Police Foundation and Policy Studies Institute

Osborn S & Shaftoe H (1995) *Safer Neighbourhoods? Successes and Failures and Crime Prevention,* London, Safe Neighbourhoods Unit

Packer H (1968) *The Limits of the Criminal Sanction,* Stanford University Press

Penal Affairs Consortium (1994) *The Case Against Secure Training Orders,* London, Penal Affairs Consortium

Penal Affairs Consortium (1995a) *The Doctrine of "Doli Incapax",* London, Penal Affairs Consortium

Penal Affairs Consortium (1995b) *The Case for a Sentencing Council,* London, Penal Affairs Consortium

Penal Affairs Consortium (1995c) *The Mandatory Life Sentence,* London, Penal Affairs Consortium

Penal Affairs Consortium (1995d) *Parental Responsibility, Youth Crime and the Criminal Law,* London, Penal Affairs Consortium

Penal Affairs Consortium (1995e) *Sentencing and Early Release: The Home Secretary's Proposals,* London, Penal Affairs Consortium

Penal Affairs Consortium (1995f) *Squatters, Travellers, Ravers, Protesters and the Criminal Law,* London, Penal Affairs Consortium

Penal Affairs Consortium (1995g) *Strengthening Punishment in the Community,* London, Penal Affairs Consortium

Pilling J (1992) *Back to Basics: Relationships in the Prison Service,* in *Perspectives on Prison: A Collection of Views on Prison Life and Running Prisons,* Supplement to the Annual Report of the Prison Service 1991-92, Cm 2087, London, HMSO

Police Foundation/Policy Studies Institute (1996) *The Role and Responsibilities of the Police,* London, Police Foundation/Policy Studies Institute

Prison Reform Trust (1993) *Report of a Committee on the Penalty for Homicide (Chairman Lord Lane of St Ippollitts),* London, Prison Reform Trust

Reiner R & Cross M (eds) (1991) *Beyond Law and Order: Criminal Justice Policy into the 1990s,* London, MacMillan

Reiner R (1992) *Policing Post-modern Society,* Modern Law Review 55/6

Reiner R (1994) *Policing and the Police* in Maguire et al, *The Oxford Handbook of Criminology,* Oxford University Press

Richardson G (1985) *The Case for Prisoners' Rights* in Maguire et al, *Accountability and Prisons,* London, Tavistock

Richardson G (1993) *Law, Process and Custody: Prisoners and Patients,* London, Weidenfeld and Nicholson

Rivara P, Shepherd J, Farrington D, Richmond P and Cannon P (1995) *Victims as Offender in Youth Violence,* Annals of Emergency Medicine, 26/5

Rose D (1996) *In the Name of the Law: The Collapse of Criminal Justice,* London, Jonathan Cape

Royal Commission on Criminal Justice (1993) Report Cm 2263, London, HMSO

Rutherford A (1992) *Growing Out of Crime: The New Era,* London, Waterside Press

Rutherford A (1996) *Transforming Criminal Policy,* Winchester, Waterside Press

Rutter M & Smith D (1995) *Psychological Disorders in Young People,* Chichester, John Wyley and Sons

Sanders A (1994a) *Thinking About Criminal Justice,* in McConville M and Bridges L (eds) *Criminal Justice in Crisis,* Aldershot, Edward Elgar

Sanders A (1994b) *From Suspect to Trial* in Maguire et al, *The Oxford Handbook of Criminology,* Oxford University Press

Schluter M and Lee D (1993) *The R-Factor,* London, Hadder and Stoughton

Shapland J, Willmore J & Duff P (1985) *Victims and the Criminal Justice System,* Aldershot, Gower

Speed M, Burrows J & Bamfield J (1995) *Retail Crime Costs: 1993/94 Survey - The Impact of Crime and the Retail Response,* Northampton, Nene College

Sparks R & Bottoms A (1995) *Legitimacy and Order in Prisons,* British Journal of Sociology, Vol 46

Snow P (1996) *White Collar Blues: A Templeton College Survey of Employee's Attitudes,* Oxford Today 8/2

Straw J (1996) *Honesty, Consistency and Progression in Sentencing: A Paper for the PLP Home Affairs Committee,* London, The Labour Party

Sutton C (1995) *Educating Parents to Cope with Difficult Children,* Health Visitor Vol 68 No. 7

Tarling R (1993) *Analysing Offending: Data, Models and Interpretations,* London, HMSO

Taylor, Lord (1993) *Speech to the Law Society in Scotland,* Reported in the Daily Telegraph 23 March 1993

Travis A (1996) *Research's Term of Probation,* The Guardian 10 April

Utting D, Bright J & Henricson C (1993) *Crime and the Family: Improving Child Rearing and Preventing Delinquency,* London, Family Policy Studies Centre

Victim Support (1993) *Compensation for Victims of Crime,* Report of an Independent Working Party, London, Victim Support

Victim Support (1995) *The Rights of Victims of Crime,* A policy paper by Victim Support, London, Victim Support

Walker N, Hough M, Lewis H (1988) *Tolerance of Leniency and Severity in England and Wales* in Walker N & Hough M (eds) *Public Attitudes to Sentencing,* Aldershot, Gower

Wallace S, Crown J, Cox A & Berger M (1995) *Health Care Needs Assessment: Child and Adolescent Mental Health,* Wessex Institute of Public Health Medicine

Wells C (1994) *Corporations and Criminal Responsibility,* Oxford, Clarendon Press

Williams G (ed) (1996) *Prisons in the Community,* St Catharines Conference Report No. 51 Windsor, King George VI and Queen Elizabeth Foundation of St Catharines

Windlesham, Lord (1993) *Responses to Crime, Volume 2, Penal Policy in the Making,* Oxford, Clarendon Press

Windlesham, Lord (1996) *Life Sentences: The Case for Assimilation,* Criminal Law Review, 1996, p250

World Health Organisation (1984) *Health of All by the Year 2000,* Copenhagen, World Health Organisation

Zedner L (1994) *Victims* in Maguire et al, *The Oxford Handbook of Criminology,* Oxford University Press

Zedner L (1995) *In Pursuit of the Vernacular: Comparing Law and Order Discourse in Britain and Germany,* Social and Legal Studies, Vol 4

Author's Biographical Note

David Faulkner is a Fellow of St John's College, Oxford, and a Senior Research Associate at the Centre for Criminological Research. He writes and lectures on various aspects of criminal justice and public administration. He is a trustee of several charities concerned with the prevention of crime and the treatment of offenders, and sits as a member of the Howard League's Council.

He served in the Home Office from 1959 until 1992, becoming Director of Operational Policy in the Prison Department in 1980, Deputy Secretary in charge of the Criminal and Research Statistics Department in 1982, and Principal Establishments Officer in 1990.

YES, I want to join the Howard League

Please complete this form and send it to
The Howard League, Freepost, 708 Holloway Rd, London N19 3BR. Charity No. 251926
(Tick membership required, please give more if you can by adding it to your banker's order and covenant)

Individual membership £35 pa ☐	Life membership £550 ☐	Unwaged £12 pa ☐
Local Group Affiliation £65 pa ☐	Corporate membership £350 pa ☐	Prisoners and families Free ☐

Please complete the banker's order and deed of covenant and return to the Howard League

- -

BANKER'S ORDER

To the Manager *(bank name and address)*

Postcode

Please pay the Howard League £ _____ every year starting on __/__/__ until further notice

Name _____ Address _____

Postcode _____

Signature _____ Bank account no. _____

Account number 00927708 at National Westminster Bank plc, PO Box 3038, 57 Victoria High Street, London SW1H OHN (Code 56 00 33). This cancels any previous order.

- -

A covenant allows the Howard League to reclaim the tax you have already paid. If you pay £35 per year, the Inland Revenue will give us an extra £11.67 - and it costs you no more.

DEED OF COVENANT

I *(name)* _____ of *(address)* _____

Postcode _____

promise to pay the Howard League during my lifetime, such a sum as after deduction of income tax at the basic rate amounts to £ _____ *(the amount of your annual payment)* per annum provided that I

may revoke in writing this deed of covenant at any time after the expiry of four years from _____
(date on which your first banker's order payment is due).

Signed and delivered *(your signature)* _____ Date _____

Witnessed by *(friend, neighbour or relative's signature)* _____

Address of witness _____

Postcode _____

- -

And/or I wish to give a donation of:

£250 ☐   £100 ☐   £50 ☐   £25 ☐   £10 ☐   Other £ _____

ONE OFF PAYMENT METHOD

Please make your cheque/postal order payable to **The Howard League, or** enter the number of your Visa/Barclaycard/Access/Mastercard/CAFcard (delete as appropriate) Expiry date __/__

No. ☐☐☐☐☐☐☐☐☐☐☐☐☐☐☐☐☐☐ Signature _____

Total Amount Enclosed £ _____
(please print clearly, if paying by credit card you should give the address where you receive your credit card bills)

Name _____ Address _____

Postcode _____ Occupation _____ Tel. _____

If you do not wish your name to be included in mailing exchanges with other like minded charities, please write to the Database Manager.

3 EASY WAYS TO JOIN THE HOWARD LEAGUE

 Telephone our Credit card hotline on 0171 281 7722, anytime from 9.30am to 5.30pm weekdays

 Complete this membership form and send it with a cheque or credit card details to: The Howard League, Freepost, 708 Holloway Rd, London N19 3BR

 Fax the completed membership form with your credit card details on 0171 281 5506